Also by Graham Williams:

Personal Power—the power that drives performance (co-author)

MIND FIT FOR SUCCESS

GRAHAM WILLIAMS

authorHOUSE®

AuthorHouse™
1663 Liberty Drive
Bloomington, IN 47403
www.authorhouse.com
Phone: 1-800-839-8640

Published by AuthorHouse   07/09/2012

ISBN: 978-1-4685-7915-4 (sc)
ISBN: 978-1-4685-7914-7 (e)

Contents

"The change that occurred was nothing short of unbelievable. Without exception, the whole team was transformed into a highly productive unit. The problems of the past have been resolved."

Chief Superintendent Tony Thomas

"I have seen many action plans work back in the workplace, but this was different. People interacted dynamically and with mutual respect"

Tony Bentley, MA (HR).
External verifying for the Institute
of Supervision and Management

"Having had little self confidence for many years I attended a Mind Fit programme where my beliefs about myself where challenged. It enabled me to recognise my abilities and personal power, this lead to the fulfilment of an ambition to work for myself. I have gone from part time employee to successful self employed international antiques dealer."

Bryony Theobald

Acknowledgements

I would like to acknowledge the following people whose contribution has made this book possible. First must be Dr Alan Beggs who I worked alongside for several years researching and developing what is now the Mind Fit process. Next is Caroline Buckley whose enthusiasm, feedback and editing has helped me along the way. Finally, Neville Gaunt whose business acumen has enabled me the time and space to research and write.

Dedication

This book is dedicated to:

Lieutenant David Alexander Grant Boyce

1st The Queen's Dragoon Guards

Killed in Afghanistan

18th September 1986 – 17th November 2011

Preface

The world has changed. Have you noticed?

The 21st century has hit us with a vengeance. Changes are occurring at an unprecedented pace. Yet are we fit to handle this change or are we still reeling under the onslaught of it?

There are many examples around us of a failure to adapt to change. For example, websites are falling behind as social media drives through the new information revolution. Yet many website builders are hanging onto the past with an unshakeable belief that websites drive people to your business. They have not accepted that people drive people these days as relationships are becoming more important and networks grow. Working in collaboration with others in a mutually supportive way, whether locally or internationally, is a major key to growing businesses. This requires an entrepreneurial mindset, not that of a traditionalist.

Classic soft skills training is also under threat. A typical example of its ineffectiveness is time management. How many people attend time management training, yet still struggle to manage time. The transfer of soft skills knowledge training into action has never been great yet it is still prophesised as the route to success. Check out the evidence.

Business consultants may know how to transform businesses through processes and systems but that was before the economic collapse of 2007. The world has changed. How many business owners or consultants are ready for today's uncertainty?

Human Resource policies, procedures and appraisal schemes do not drive performance or change. They should support it. People who have a purpose, are engaged and have passion drive performance and change.

The new reality

When the environment is relatively stable, the traditional approaches thrive. When it changes rapidly innovators and entrepreneurs, who often live on the edge, expand. Today, the worldwide changes to the economic environment suggest that most of the innovators and entrepreneurs are in the emerging countries. They are clear examples of how people who have lived on the edge are now the forerunners of dynamic new economies. The old traditional economic environment is struggling and stagnating.

Many business people are putting their heads in the sand waiting for the return to a past world where they were the leaders in their field. It is time to stop waiting. The time to change is here now. You can either embrace it or struggle on. The good news is that all of us have the innate assets to change and meet the challenges.

Businesses that fail to adapt will likely die out or, at very best, struggle to survive. The business news is full of such stories of struggling companies whether they are major high tech organisations, camera and film manufacturers or long established holiday firms who continue to seek financial support. The public sector in the UK is a clear example of an organisation that has failed to adapt in a meaningful way for years. It now has to make severe cuts to the services provided and staff. How we operate is also being challenged as some of the larger players like Enron and News International have recently discovered.

This is why becoming Mind Fit is crucial if you are going to survive in the chaos and complexity that has been left by the economic collapse. The evidence that entrepreneurs are making a difference is all around us. Open your eyes and you will see people who are making inroads into new areas; some are creating something new, others are diversifying whilst a few have upped their game. Traditional businesses may bounce back for a while, but in the long run we all need to learn to adapt to change because change is constant.

We can all change, adapt and become entrepreneurial. Neuroscience is informing us how the brain is malleable and therefore can change and grow. We do not have to be stuck in our old habits based on old beliefs of how to do things. We are not what we believe we are. We are more. We have a huge capacity to grow. We can change our beliefs. We can change our personality. We can develop new personal strengths. We can become Mind Fit.

If we are going to change: where to start? We must not lose the learning from the past. We need to take that learning and adopt 21st century methods of development.

Some people have already changed and we can learn from them. They needed to do something different to both survive and thrive in their businesses. What caused them to change is the economic climate. This may not have been by choice but out of necessity to survive.

Mind Fitness

This book is about using our innate assets in a dynamic way, to adapt to the challenges by using action based natural learning to make those changes, rather than through knowledge alone. It is an innovative approach to adjusting to an unpredictable future. It is the first step, the entry point that we all need to take to be successful. It is about becoming Mind Fit. Mind Fitness leads to positive actions, to growth, to business improvement. This applies whether you are a small business owner or an employee in a large multi-national.

Doing what we have always done will no longer get us the results that we have always got. The world has changed. So must we. Innovators and entrepreneurs have the ability to adjust to changes by reinventing themselves over and over again in what they do and how they do it. We all have the innate ability to change. We first have to believe it and take action.

Mind Fitness enables a person to perform to their optimum for the benefit of a desired outcome, whether personal or for the business.

One important message to start with. Developing Mind Fitness is not training. The approach does not give people knowledge. The process, which this book outlines, is as different to training as chalk is to cheese. Actions drive Mind Fitness, not knowledge. Mind Fitness drives an innovative and entrepreneurial mindset.

This is a radical new approach which is terrifying many traditionalists in business and people development. Many of those people that have been delivering the same products with the same systems and the same development programmes for decades are struggling. They act as if nothing has really changed. The old thinking, methods and programmes that rarely delivered what clients wanted in the past, will make even less of an impact now.

Mind Fitness is an innovative approach enabling people to change positively, quickly and willingly. It has one very clear aim: to revolutionise people's performance, and that of the business that they are in or want to build. The approach is both very primitive, which enabled our forebears to survive in hostile and changing environments, yet innovative and 21st century. The gems from the past are linked to some of the latest understanding from psychology, biology, epigenetic, neuroscience and neuroplasticity.

Although science underpins the material in this book, it is very clearly aimed at a down to earth explanation of how we operate as human beings, some of which are positive whilst other ways can be self destructive. You will easily recognise in an intuitive way many of the descriptions that are given in this book in both yourself and others, and the impact that it can have on businesses and our lives.

This book will provide you with intriguing insights, a Personal Profile Map® and introduce you to the core method used to increase Mind Fitness so that you can become an innovator, an entrepreneur and deliver effective performance. It is also a life skill.

Developing Mind Fitness is the prequel to action rather than the traditional approach of giving people knowledge first and hope that they take action back in the workplace. With a 'can do' mindset people change their beliefs, attitudes and behaviours and choose willingly to act.

Putting the record straight

Knowledge is beneficial if it is relevant, accurate and useable. The key here is useable. If it is not, then it is a waste of time, effort and money in a business sense. It may be appropriate for personal development but the focus here is to develop people who are agile, adaptable and flexible to meet the challenges of today's new world.

Mind Fitness does however, when combined with the relevant and useable knowledge, generates in people a sense of Personal Power. Without it people often operate with a 'can't do' or 'won't do' attitude. Mind Fitness produces 'can do' people: those innovators and entrepreneurs. Mind Fit people will seek out the knowledge they need when they need it. Not when someone else says they need it.

This book will pull apart the different components of Mind Fitness and explore some of the elements which sit beneath and behind it. It will challenge many of the traditional myths that are regularly expounded by many business consultants and trainers.

The biggest obstacle to discovering something new is the belief that you already know it.

CHAPTER 1

Mind Fitness

Quote: 'There is nothing good or bad, but thinking makes it so.' Hamlet, Act II, scene ii

Building a successful business

The traditional approach to building a successful business favoured by many people who work in or support organisations, is that all you need are two parts of the puzzle shown below—Business Fit and Knowledge Fit. The fact that people are involved seems to have been ignored.

First, the components that ensure a business is fit include: vision and mission, a strategy, a business plan with goals and targets, finance, health and safety, HR and training. To implement the plan employees need to have the relevant skills and knowledge so that they are Knowledge Fit. It is simply a matter of connecting the two parts of the jigsaw together, around an organisational structure, policies and procedures, and let it happen.

Unfortunately, experience tells us it has never worked as well as it should have done. For decades people have been tweaking these two component parts of the jigsaw in an attempt to improve the strength of each and the join that separates them. The missing part of the puzzle, Mind Fitness, has been ignored.

The fact is that today, even after decades of business modelling and training, we still have unacceptable high levels of underperformance, disengagement, stress and conflict at work. Leadership is often criticised and the complexity of working in teams seems to defy explanation. This clearly demonstrates that the adoption and implementation of these various business plans and training inputs are not being actioned in the most effective ways. And in most cases, it is people who do the actioning. People are not that simple.

Neither is the environment simple that businesses and people operate in, particularly today. All of us and the world we live and work in are more complex than most of us can imagine. But there is a solution. Because, like any complex system which the world of work is, there are patterns which can enable us to predict to some degree how things might work and how people might operate. But first it requires putting in place the missing part of the jigsaw: Mind Fitness.

What is Mind Fitness?

Mind Fitness is a learned ability to operate effectively across all component parts of the mind thus enabling a person to perform to their optimum for the benefit of a desired outcome.

The process is action based not knowledge learning. The learning that takes place is natural rather than educational. Knowledge is obviously crucial but as you will see, it stands apart from being Mind Fit although linked.

The Mind Fit process uses those parts of the brain that we have some control over and impact on our lives. Previously, we have spent decades, in fact centuries, focused on academic learning as the key to success. Having knowledge does not always lead to what you desire. I was introduced to a delightful lady at a university graduation ceremony of a friend. I learnt that the lady had a first degree, a Masters, a PhD and an MBA plus numerous other qualifications. Yet she could not keep a job. She became completely overwhelmed by the belief that she did not have sufficient knowledge and had to keep learning. She was emotionally out of control and her thought processes were irrational.

To become Mind Fit a person needs to be in control of and develop practical strengths in those four core components of the brain relevant to Mind Fitness. These are:

1. Thinking self—the ability to think flexibly and focus appropriately

How much of our day to day thinking is focused on what we do or need to do in a work context? Is it on improving what we do and how we do it? Is it on our performance or is it unfocused and therefore unproductive? Unfocused, inappropriate and inadequate thinking can lead to rigid thinking, paralysis of action and underperformance. For example, a sales person may not pick up the phone to make a call or a leader may avoid tackling a dispute between two members of staff. How often do you drift off into 'another' place when driving your car or get involved in a conversation about something irrelevant when you should be concentrating?

Learning to think flexibly and appropriately in different situations by using a selection of practical tools will provide a thought-out solution enabling actions to follow.

2. Feeling self—to be emotionally competent and resilient

Surprisingly, although we are often very aware of other people's emotions, many of us are not that aware of our own until they become an extreme, either positive or negative. We often get locked into feelings of negativity and have learnt some simple unconscious techniques to stay in that state such as apathy or frustration. This is not only unproductive it can be personally damaging. If we can learn naturally to stay in a negative state then it is not difficult to learn naturally to stay in a positive state.

Becoming aware of and taking control of emotions will lead to a much more enjoyable and fulfilled life. We also bounce back quicker from negativity.

3. Driving self—to be committed with a real sense of purpose

I call this our driving self because many of the facets found in this part of our mind operate at a semiconscious or unconscious level. The driving self is the 'engine' room that drives us. It includes beliefs, expectations, motivators and values. Many are difficult to put into words without exploring the meaning behind what drives us. They do however add richness to our very being. They are our motivators, our code of conduct, and produce our unique character. Pulling them into our conscious mind enables us to discard those beliefs that are not true or block actions. For example, by learning how to challenge negative beliefs about ourself and change them, we can become a more grounded person able to operate in an authentic way. Knowing what our drivers are and how we seek to satisfy them in a work context can be very rewarding.

Our attitudes are formed in this part of ourself. I am of the opinion that negative attitudes cause clashes, not our personality. Our attitudes can make or break relationships. But, like our personality, they can change.

4. **Social self—the ability to connect meaningfully with others**

To achieve this we have to learn to accept people for who they are or believe they are. This is different from so many situations where people decide for whatever reason that they do not like someone. We can use language and behaviours that build relationships rather than destroy them. We can be open-minded, we can keep quiet. We can learn to have dialogue and not argue. We can learn to inspire, involve and engage. Who would not want this type of person as a team member or leader?

Developing our social self enables us to live in a positive way and build solid relationships or relationships that develop a business. Business success in the future will require an enhancement of our ability to build and sustain relationships.

Mind Fitness leads to increased performance

Once a person starts the journey to become Mind Fit, the information and insights they receive enables them to self assess. Self assessment is one of the core parts of the Mind Fit process. Rather than push knowledge in, people start to look inwardly at themselves. Not only do they identify the strengths and weaknesses in other people, that explain why people do what they do, but they start to assess their own capabilities in all the component parts of Mind Fitness. This is a real eye opener as they start to discover why they do what they do. Now individuals have a choice.

All that is subsequently needed to kick start the process off is a small change which often leads to big impact. It is like rolling a snowball downhill. The first revolution will gather a small amount of snow. The second a bit more, and by the tenth revolution the snowball will have gained considerably in size. By the bottom of the hill it could be massive. To ensure the process works, people commence making personal changes by taking a small action within 24 hours of any input. As they build their confidence, the changes are linked to the business needs. This ensures that their performance leads directly to increased productivity.

Let us not forget knowledge. Mind Fitness, when combined with the relevant knowledge, generates a sense of Personal Power. In essence, it provides the confidence, resilience and courage to act. Without Mind Fitness and knowledge people are easily distracted, often avoid focusing on what they should be doing and continually seek to justify why they are not performing to their optimum.

Distracted Mary

Mary, who worked for a local authority, was suffering from stress. She consistently took three hours a day to perform a financial task required by her director. This task reduced her time to complete other parts of her own job. She was under pressure. She felt very stressed and had regular bouts of sickness. Following a one day Mind Fit workshop she simply identified those small distracters which were either totally or partially in her control, and stopped doing them. First, she switched off the 'peep' when an email entered her inbox. She informed her colleagues when she was not to be disturbed even though it was an open planned office, and she learnt how to focus better. With a few other small tweaks the three hour task was swiftly reduced to one hour a day. Problem solved.

Some of you might be thinking that this is too easy. But it really is how it works. Tasks are completed much quicker if you apply focused effort on what is important instead of being constantly distracted, internally and eternally, or keep prevaricating. Next time you want to complete something, become aware of what you actually do.

What is different about the process?

The difference that builds Mind Fitness, leads to increased performance, and what makes it different from knowledge learning, are shown below in these four key points:

- The importance of using the whole brain and not just the cognitive or educated parts.

- The power of using natural (implicit) learning as opposed to educated (explicit) learning.

- A Personal Profile Map®, which has been constructed from the gems of many theories. The map helps people to self assess and make choices.

- Identifying existing personal strengths and discover how to develop new ones and turn them into actions.

Global strengths

This book will constantly remind you of the importance of the four global strengths that form the foundation in every area of every action that is needed to develop Mind Fitness linked to increasing performance. They are:

- **Awareness**—most people's 'map' of themselves and others is full of holes or may contain some fundamental errors. By continually increasing our awareness we can choose to make changes.

- **Control**—people with a positive and flexible mind have considerable internal and personal control. Those who are easily overwhelmed or have a sense of vulnerability don't.

- **Focus**—to change and improve what you do requires focused effort on what is really important and the ability to be distracted less often.

- **Feedback**—seek immediate feedback from whatever source is available. This enables an increase in awareness. The process now becomes cyclical.

As you discover that you can take personal control around these global strengths and understand what they do, you will discover more of your own existing strengths. Your confidence will grow so that you then start identifying and building new strengths. This benefits both yourself and your organisation as you become more agile and adapable.

This new, holistic and unique process takes people on a journey of personal discovery called Learned Powerfulness®. It is a scientifically sound process, yet simple and practical. It is both personal and business focused. The crucial difference to the Mind Fit approach is that I quite deliberately do not give participants theories or knowledge as a means to develop, neither do I want people to adopt a cognitive approach to learning. The process is pulling out those innate assets, building on them and applying them.

Evaluation of the process

One of the reasons the process is sustainable is because it is built on naturally learning; in the same way we learned to ride a bike. Natural learning is inherently very sustainable. Can you still ride a bike? And how many of the myriad facts we learned at school can we still remember? You can learn naturally to become more resilient, courageous, imaginative or a relationship builder. You can become an innovator and entrepreneur.

Natural learning enables us to undertake a vast amount of our daily activities without conscious thought. Things like cleaning our teeth, getting dressed, or driving a car all become effortless after some practice. This form of learning occurs deep inside our minds and is achieved through experiences, copying, visualising, by accident and the experience of occasional 'aha' moments. As well as the mundane low-level behaviours which get us through our day, natural learning helps form our attitudes and mindsets. In truth, we are all creatures of habit, both physical and psychological.

Natural learning is unconscious and automatic. It enables us to handle the complexity of ourself, others and different situations. When used in a deliberate and focused way, performance keeps improving.

We just need to do it.

CHAPTER 2

The Business Case
for Mind Fitness

Quote: 'We hire people for their technical skills and knowledge, and fire them for their attitude.' Source unknown

What has Mind Fitness got to do with business?

'Sounds like a lot of soft fluffy stuff. I've got better things to do with my time so why should I waste it on Mind Fitness? I've seen it all before. Nothing you can teach me. Running a business is simple. Tell people what you want them to do and if they don't do it, they have a choice'.

I come across this type of mindset so often. Some business owners, managers and team leaders seem to have such a limited understanding of what makes a business develop and grow. Staff can also have very fixed views that impact on business potential. 'I'm here just to earn money. I keep my head down and get on with it. Don't want to get involved'. Others do get involved wherever they can, but not in a productive way. They are awkward to deal with, will block new initiatives, make a lot of noise and look for fault in everyone else. Strongly opinionated, these people can stop business growth effortlessly and cause mayhem in the process.

People are the business. Businesses today need to have living and dynamic strategies, plans, policies and procedures in place but on their own they are meaningless.

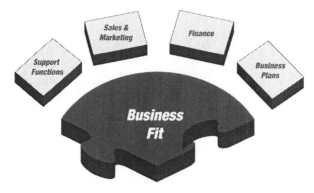

Business consultants can quickly identify what is going wrong and provide a plan and process to build success. Lean management and financial plans are examples of this. Do they work? In some businesses, such interventions do not get off the ground. In others they do help organisations, but for how long? In recent times a leading Japanese car manufacturer's lean process got into trouble. It has cost them a fortune to replace parts in cars across the world as well as a major dent into customer confidence and satisfaction. Could it be that they have forgotten that people are involved?

People do need to have the relevant knowledge linked to the plan to make the business work. But both of those aspects have been in place for years yet performance and productivity problems still exist in running a business. A fortune has been spent on consultancy and training people, yet it is the mindset, the attitudes, of people that create many of the problems that exist in organisations.

Trainers provide knowledge that they perceive is appropriate to meet the organisations current or future needs. In the area of technical knowledge, this works quite well. But this is not the case when it comes to some of the softer training such as leadership, team working, change and personal effectiveness. Once again experience and reality tells us that it is not that simple to turn knowledge into action. Research and evidence informs us that current theory or concept based training consistently fails to change attitude and behaviours or deliver tangible results as predicted by training companies. As many of us have discovered, on returning to work after soft training input, a majority of people soon resume their old working practices.

The link between knowledge input, relating to these soft areas of training, and action back in the workplace has been described as random chance. Soft training is not working to the level of the promises made by providers. This is why it is time to adopt a different approach to meet the new economic challenges which will generate the drive for change. That is the third part of the jigsaw and we will explore the various parts that make up this piece.

However, before we move on I must reiterate that it is important that the business and knowledge parts of the jigsaw are critical, and appropriate time and effort must be given to both.

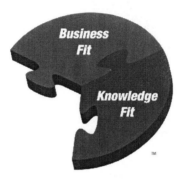

We also need to recognise that people that operate within organisations are not simple systems that participate in fixed structures or procedures that can be directed and expected to perform in a predetermined way. Although logic suggests that is what will happen, experience tells us it does not. It may happen for a while, but eventually things will go wrong.

The reality

One of the biggest problems is obvious. It is people. But people are also the solution to business growth. If you want people to become an integral part of business and the development and growth of that business, then it is time to recognise that people are complex beings. Our obsolete linear approach to developing people, often driven by business consultants, Human Resources (HR) and training needs to change. People are not robots who just function at our beck and call. Neither are we simple logical beings that conform. We are very complex yet there is a pattern to this complexity which I will unravel later in the book and which is intuitively obvious. First, here is an example of a small business that acknowledged the complexity of working together in a difficult economic climate, and set down some basic rules on how to operate.

The print company

This is a family start up business I deal with. The economy was collapsing, not just in the UK but worldwide, yet they decided to start a digital print business. The area the business was being set up in was already flooded with print companies providing everything from business cards to massive displays for exhibitions.

They had one printing machine and knew very little about printing. Yet they still set out to build a business. Acquiring the knowledge and learning about the technology and its capability was relatively simple. Putting together a business and finance plan and all the other facets of a business to ensure that it was **Business Fit** were put into place. Not difficult with a small business. They explored the market, their competitors and their likely customers. They conducted a reality check. They looked at cost and potential profit which is all very sensible. They identified the breakeven point.

In addition, they considered what each member of the family could contribute and what they wanted out of the business because this is the area where potential conflicts can occur. They knew that they would have to develop new strengths to meet new job roles to make it work. That did not faze them. They became **Knowledge Fit**. This family has a real 'can do' attitude.

Before they started they identified five promises to their customers which to this day are still the driving principles behind the business. They worked hard. They learnt their trade and they found customers. Slowly at first. The business kept growing. Customers stayed. All key decisions were made by the family through a shared process.

In the last three years they have moved premises twice and keep investing in new machines. The business has a real sense of purpose. They have increased staff and doubled their annual turnover year in year out. Their customers remain loyal.

I became one of their customers. What they said they would do they did. They are pleasant and very customer focused. They really listen to what you want and spend time working with you to design exactly what you need. They are people focused.

My contribution to this business has been small. I have spent time with them talking about Mind Fitness, its tools and techniques. The Managing Director found that discovering how to focus on what is really important saved him a huge amount of time, effort and money. They are without a doubt innovative and entrepreneurial. They listen to what their customers want, they keep their eyes open for new opportunities and this is evident by the new services that they are consistently making. The atmosphere is always welcoming.

This all took place whilst other print companies are struggling to survive or were going out of business. The difference is that in this business they also worked at becoming **Mind Fit**.

Learning from evolution

The print company operates in an environment where there are limited customers and a lot of competitors, yet they are thriving. Human evolution can inform us a lot about how people act today and why some thrive and some go out of business.

This might seem rather bizarre but imagine living many thousands of years ago in a hostile environment on the edge of a forest where you sometimes venture into a more open landscape to hunt. The trees provide some degree of security whilst the open space encourages various herbivores to live. They in turn provide an essential food supply. It is a hostile environment where you can move from hunter to hunted in the blink of an eye. Our earlier ancestors and other anatomically different humans existed in such a harsh environment. We were then and still are today at the mercy of environmental change.

Those early ancestors that stuck to what they always did were safe when the environment was relatively stable. But when change occurred, the evidence is that all other human species of which there have been several vanished except our forebears. Those others human species were as competent and large brained as we are today. Yet they died out. Why?

Change occurred. Woodlands retreated or expanded. Prey moved or vanished. Species succumbed to either the rapid rise in temperatures leading to a more desert environment or a decrease resulting in the extremely cold and harsh world of the tundra. These events were repeated many times over ten of thousands of millennia.

One member of those early ancestors did survive—us. We survived because we adapted. We took the learning from the past, moved away from the edge of the forest which had been our home and developed new hunting tools and techniques. We started to co-operate in larger groups and to share expertise. That ability to adapt then does not mean we are immune to change. Like those other human species that died out we also get comfortable with our environment and do not want to change. The economic environment is today's environmental challenge. Are we ready for it?

Why do organisations need Mind Fitness?

Are we ready for change? The short answer is 'no' for many people and organisations. I have worked with a wide range of organisations from high Tech to low Tech, from public and private sectors, and from shop floor to chief executives. Many people in those organisations were, to varying degrees, mind UN-Fit. They functioned at a comfortable level, doing what they had always done. They were not focused on business performance, nor really involved or concerned about the organisation. Many were not focused on people. There was no drive, nor response to potential changes that were happening.

They just kept doing what they did. The businesses were run in traditional ways which had worked in the past, but were not adapting to the new economic world disorder. These people were not Mind Fit and the businesses were not Business Fit. And this misshaped jigsaw part will not fit into the whole puzzle.

Here are a few simple examples of wasted time, effort and money:

- The leader who allowed a project manager to take five days off before she started new projects so she could get her mind right. She handles ten projects a year. I pointed out that she was in fact working 50 days, or ten weeks, a year less than other members of the team and it was causing conflict. He allowed this unacceptable time wasting because he did not know what to do.

- The manager of a series of production lines in a manufacturing company refused to talk to team members if he did not like them. Messages had to be directed through a third person. People just said that was the way he was. It caused confusion and delays, and underperformance.

- In a factory where one of the machines could not meet the demand of throughput, the workforce, who were constantly shouted at by aggressive directors and managers, devised a system which made it appear that the developing product was moving from one machine to the next along the production line was in constant motion. In fact, the employees kept the parts going round in circles so it was an illusion and a time waster.

- In a major airline, the loaders always got the blame when they failed to complete the loading of an aircraft within the time slot allocated for turn around. It created an unpleasant atmosphere and strike action was always looming. The problem, when investigated, was in fact caused in the baggage handling hall by machines that were old and kept breaking down. No one had checked.

Imagine this sort of poor performance across your organisation.

The big picture

Time wasting is only one problem. There are many more issues that impact on performance and productivity.

Let's have a look at some of them. The fact that stress at work, lack of engagement, conflict, grievances and underperformance is routinely reported as major issues from a variety of professional bodies and other sources from around the world, shows there is a major problem. The problems have existed for years.

The cost to businesses as a result of these factors is unbelievable. Underperformance has been quoted as costing the UK economy £70 billion pounds a year. Add the cost of stress and the other factors to this and the sums become astronomical.

Gallup's biannual survey relating to engagement at work suggests that up to 79% of the workforce in the UK is disengaged, passively or actively. But this is not restricted to the UK. It is a worldwide phenomenon. Some recent global figures issued by Gallup in 2011 are 17, 300, 16000. They state that 17% of the workforce is 'actively' disengaged, which relates to $300 billion dollars lost at a cost of $16000 a year for each disengaged employee. What about the 'passively' disengaged?

There is also an acknowledged threat to the German economy from information provided by Gallup in their journal in June 2011. This states that only 13% of German employees are engaged. The economy may seem robust but there appears to be a significant reduction in confidence caused by regional and global factors which make it vulnerable. For example, the Euro crises, the flagging U.S. economy and the cooling of China's manufacturing economy.

One report suggested that managers can spend 13% of their time dealing with underperformance and 14% of time correcting the mistakes those people have generated.

At shop floor level, an IT company did their own research in the UK and found that the average person working in the profession was only engaged 60% of their time working on their job. However; only 70% of that time was working efficiently. This means that the average person was focused on their job for 3.1 hours per day. On a £30,000 per annum salary, which equates £16.43p per hour on a 3.1 hour focused day, the employees true cost is £88.93p per hour. That does take into account other factors including holidays, training and sick leave.

One other figure I came across was that misery cost £3038 per person. However, it is not all doom and gloom. There are some engaged employees out there who are performing.

Here are some figures relating to engaged employees:

- 25% more productive in a restaurant.

- Between 12% and 70% more productive.

- Put in 10% more discretionary effort.

- Take three times less sick leave.

- Stay in their job five times longer.

- Are 10 times more energised.

Mind Fit people are engaged people and performance focused. How can anyone in business not want to be engaged or have engaged employees?

Do you want this?   Or this?

Current remedies

A lot of effort has been put into finding the remedies for those factors which have such a big impact on performance and productivity. In the UK the cost of training has been put at £33 billion. Initiatives by government, professional bodies, training companies and a myriad of individual trainers have pronounced solutions to these issues for years. But they have in the main not delivered what they promise.

One example is sickness and stress at work. There has been a reduction in the number of stress cases over the last decade. However, it is still too high. The Health and Safety Executive for Great Britain regularly publishes statistics. The figures for 2009/10 showed the number of new cases of work-related stress had reduced to 211,000 from 233,000 over a 10 year period but this was also reported by them as not statistically significant.

In terms of total working days lost during 2010/2011 it was reported as 10.8 million days off, which has reduced from 12.9 million days since 2001.

My point is that during the first decade of the 21ˢᵗ century a huge amount of time, money and effort has been expended yet the problem still remains enormous. HR, training and other providers have sought to tackle the problem.

Examples of training programmes currently provided for tackling stress include:

- Stress management.

- Coping with stress.

- How to deal with stress as leaders.

- Identifying the signs of stress.

- Interviewing people returning to work.

They have not worked very well. There is another way. Instead of tackling the symptoms of underperformance, disengagement, sickness, stress, conflict and grievances, we should tackle the cause: mind UN-Fitness. When a person feels energised, confident, resilient and pro-active these symptoms go. Mind Fit people rarely suffer from these states.

Mind Fitness is about people and performance. Instead of approaching the problem from a negative perspective it is tackled from a positive mindset. Get your mindset right and then work related issues are significantly reduced or vanish.

The team from hell

A public sector team of 28 people was causing major problems. It was one of six teams in the organisation all providing the same service yet it was significantly underperforming and was in fact the worst amongst all the teams. There were two cases of stress at work, several ongoing grievances under formal investigation and more were in the pipeline. Conflict was rife. It was not a pleasant place to work.

HR, training and mediation had all been attempted without success. Acknowledging the issues that existed within the team I immediately moved on to developing Mind Fitness, its links to teams and performance. A total of three and a half days input took place over three months which required participants to take small actions each time to improve their Mind Fitness, how it relates to others and performance. Behavioural ground rules were identified.

After three months the result was a totally different team. The team was transformed. All the issues had been resolved and the team had become the top performing team in the organisation. Engagement measures taken before the intervention by the organisation were repeated afterwards and found improvements of between 50% and 100%.

The senior person for the organisation stated:

'This was a team that was totally dysfunctional and nobody knew what to do. Various professionals and specialists had been involved and people had been sent on a variety of training courses. None of this made any noticeable difference. I was aware of what (Mind Fitness) does and knew that it was a unique and dynamic process with positive results. I recommended the process to the management and specialist team and a meeting was held between them to discuss the team and the problems they were causing.

'Our expectations were low as all previous methods had made no noticeable impact. The change that occurred between December 2010 and March 2011 was nothing short of unbelievable. Without exception, the whole team was transformed into a highly productive unit. The problems of the past had been resolved and what's remarkable is that there remains a determination to continue their on-going successes. Several months after the programme was completed the team still hold regular sessions to discuss what is happening within the team and within the organisation. They proactively discuss any issues that might impact on them and their performance. They are open and supportive and issues are resolved professionally.'

Tomorrow starts today

Evolution tells us that traditionalists respond to climate and environmental change by sticking to their preferred way of life. They do not like change and will do their utmost to stay the same. Burying our head in the sand to the reality around us does not help. The world has changed forever. We can be like those early ancestors, those with a more traditional view of the world, who died out as they waited for the old stable environment to return. Or we can do something about it. We can become energised, innovative and entrepreneurial, and adapt to the changes.

The time to change is now. History informs us of this. Organisations can no longer afford to have underperforming people from whatever cause if they are going to survive and then thrive. Organisations need to change. People need to change; they need to become Mind Fit. This includes teams and leaders. Mind Fitness permeates through everyone and every role. It is critical to improving performance.

First though, we need to understand what we mean by performance.

CHAPTER 3

Performance

Quote: 'Performance is not simply a matter of how capable one is, but how capable one believes oneself to be.' Pajares 2002

Before we unpick Mind Fitness in depth we need to explore what performance is. This book is in the main about people performing at work although Mind Fitness is also a life skill. Its intention is to encourage people to make small personal changes in what they do and how they do it. These changes, linked to the business, can revolutionise performance.

What is performance?

I have asked hundreds and hundreds of people this question over the years and still today I have not had a consistent answer. I have seen many blank faces from people who are supposedly professionals in the field of personal and business performance. I also get a variety of answers that include performance is what you achieve, meeting your targets through to what you are currently doing. I find this amazing because underperformance is known to be a major issue with people at work today. One source I referred to earlier suggests that underperformance cost the UK economy more than £70 billion pounds a year. This exceeds significantly the cost to the economy of conflict and stress at work.

Food for thought

In the previous chapter, I referred to some research from the IT world that suggests the amount of focused time applied by people working actually on their job, as being an average of 3.1 hours a day.

- 3.1 hours is probably high for some organisations. How much time each day do you actually focus on an aspect of your role which is directly or indirectly linked to performance and productivity?

- What impact would an extra hour of focused time a day make to your business?

Back to the beginning. If we cannot agree what performance is, how can we hope to improve it?

A sports view

I want to share with you my experience when I worked with former top performing sports people, albeit in the business arena. They were a mix of athletes, a racing driver, coaches and sports psychologist. They had a very clear understanding of what performance is and what it is not.

Performance for the sports professionals I have spoken too was clearly based on what they did at a moment in time. What they actually achieved, the output, is the result of those many small actions in real time that add up to improving their results and perhaps winning.

Imagine you are a one hundred metre sprinter. You have walked up to the start line and you are about to get ready to run. Where is your focus?

When I asked this question I was expecting the athletes to say winning. I was wrong. They had already set a dream goal of bursting over the finish line first and standing on the podium with a gold medal. They had also set a realistic end goal with a personal time target they needed to beat. Their focus at the beginning of the race was now on what they were about to do. Where they placed their feet in the blocks, then the focus shifted to where they placed their hands along the start line. Next, getting their body poised, listening for the 'B' of the bang. Their focus instantly changes to powering out of the blocks, getting their stride right, placing their feet down in the way that gives them the best spring and drive. If they do all the little things right, which is in their control, they will increase their chance of beating their own time. What they cannot control are the other seven participants who will also be seeking to do the same. They told me that focus on the opponents' leads to losing. It is the wrong focus.

The chance of winning is only likely to happen if they get all the small inputs right, in the right sequence, at the right moment, on that day. This is what performance means to them. If it did not work that time, they sought feedback on which of the small inputs they needed to focus on to improve their performance in the future. They became more aware, learnt from the experience and moved on.

When this principal is applied to business, the result of making small positive changes to what and how you do things, will ultimately lead to achieving set targets and improving productivity. It puts you in control of your actions. Collectively in a team or in an organisation this can make a big impact. Focusing on the input helped the small printing company described earlier to grow.

In organisational terms, getting all the small inputs right relating to sales, lean processes, excellent customer service, exceptional leadership or dynamic team working leads to an increase in productivity, or service and efficiency, and ultimately for some, profit.

If you do not consciously know what the small inputs are, how can you change and improve.

Business performance

One of the biggest mistakes that businesses consistently make is to only focus on the output, those desired targets that they set. There is nothing wrong with this if everyone involved from the top team to the operatives know clearly what they need to do at the input level to achieve those outputs. Setting a target is fine. Understanding how to achieve it through those small inputs is crucial.

The sales team

A sales team in a well established company has recently set a new target of a 20% increase in productivity to take place over the next three years. The top team have told their sales people that if they fail to meet the new targets they will receive a reduction in pay. Neither the top team nor the sales staff had explored how to achieve this target. Many of you will recognise this common approach which is based on an organisational reward and punishment mindset which unfortunately, is still thriving today even though it has been known for decades that it is self destructive. The organisation has unknowingly sabotaged its own likelihood of success. It may achieve some improvement but it is unlikely to be sustainable as there are no foundations.

I can imagine the frustration behind why the top team has instigated this approach. All they are after is an increase in performance and productivity. Who isn't? The way they are going about it will, in all probability, create a culture based on fear and vulnerability. The sales team in question are experienced, all sell the same products and were recruited because their psychological profile fitted what the organisation wanted of a sales person.

Logic suggests that if everyone has virtually the same profile, and the relevant sales and product knowledge, together with similar experience, then they should be performing to similar levels. Unfortunately this is not happening.

Success will only be achieved by everyone operating from a Mind Fit position and taking an innovative approach. Part of that approach is to identify all those little things that sales people do to obtain sales. This company needs to stop being a traditional organisation and become innovative and entrepreneurial. Their world has changed. Their customer base will also be changing because of the economy. They do not seem to understand that it has.

The manufacturing company

This company produced white goods. The top team had decided to double production using the same equipment with the same mindset, demanding the employees work harder. This failed. Instead an aggressive climate grew which made matters worse. The company was heading for bankruptcy.

I was asked to intervene. The first task was to change people's beliefs and attitude so that everyone was operating from a 'can do' mindset. Staff had to be fully involved and engaged in the challenges that the organisation faced. What the workforce on the shop floor had to contribute would ultimately lead to success. First, they needed the top team to listen. I negotiated this with the top team on their behalf.

Time was initially spent getting the workforce Mind Fit. Then, individually and in teams, they were tasked to identify small input changes that they could make to improve performance and increase productivity.

An amazing number of new actions were identified linked to input performance which increased productivity from 55 units a week to 85 units over three months. The only reason it could not be improved further was that one of the production machines had reached its maximum output level of components. This knowledge enabled the directors to make an informed decision as to the future based on the facts now available and not a wish list.

How was it done?

Production was improved through some very practical actions identified by individuals and teams. These included such methods as:

- An additional hole was placed at a corner of each unit panel allowing a hook to be temporarily inserted. This enabled a second row of panels to be hooked on to the first. Two rows of panels could now pass through the paint shop on the conveyor belt in one go. It doubled the throughput, saved time and reduced the amount of paint used.

- A temporary store was set up within the workshop where all completed sections were taken. This resulted in a reduction in time caused by looking for the relevant part around the factory.

- Stores ensured that sufficient parts were placed in bins for the assembly workers at the start of each production line.

- A store of tools and other equipment requested by the night shift was placed in a readily accessible box preventing people conducting unnecessary and time wasting searches within the store.

- An electrical loom was developed which could be fitted into each refrigeration unit direct from the workbench, reducing fitting time from 2 hours 10 minutes to 45 minutes per unit.

- Tests were carried out on each piece of machinery to ascertain the reality of its capability. This helped in the planning process.

- Each drawing was re-examined to find out how accurate it was and to identify where changes had to be made. This reduced waste in metal bent incorrectly through inaccurate drawings, saving considerable time and money.

- Each unit was taken off the production line after 45 minutes, which was the time set for completion. The incomplete ones went into a 'hospital' area for finishing. Every reason for not completing the unit within the given time was examined. This lead to a complete picture of where the delays were caused in the factory and why. It prevented blame being used for failure to complete a unit and enabled improved planning to overcome the delays.

- Transport was integrated into the manufacturing process to ensure that the completed units were wrapped and loaded for shipment to customers earlier.

A total of 45 actions were instigated by the team leaders.

Some of these solutions seem obvious from the outside but for those engaged in the process and operating in a mind UN-Fit environment improving performance and coming up with new solutions was the last thing on their mind.

Success came through people discovering that they already had what it takes to be Mind Fit. All that was needed then was to empower those people on the production line to solve the problems and seek new ways of working. They became innovators and entrepreneurs. The company survived.

How many performance improvement measures could you come up with in your organisation?

My description of performance

It is nothing fancy. Chaos and complexity theory informs us that small changes have big impacts. Those small changes need to be made at the input end. Therefore: 'Performance is the ability to identify the small task actions that lead to success, learn to focus on those actions, and take action.'

If you do not know what you do to get the results that you get, then how can you improve?

Mind Fit strengths

To identify those small success actions and take action requires four global strengths that become embedded in all you do. You have already been introduced to these strengths which are crucial in everything we do, particularly when performing. They are:

- **Awareness**—most people's 'map' of themselves and others is full of holes or may contain some fundamental errors about who they are and how they operate. Biology and neuroscience informs us that 95% of our decisions, actions, emotions and behaviours are driven from a subconscious level. In other words we do what we do without thinking. By increasing our awareness, by thinking and challenging what we do, including our beliefs, we can take more control of our self and make those changes that we choose to make.

- **Control**—people with confidence are resilient and have a positive and flexible mind, are Mind Fit. They have considerable internal and personal control. They have developed the capacity to learn from past experiences, to identify a future they want, and they know how to focus on the moment to improve performance in all that they do. If they cannot control something they know how to let go.

- **Focus**—to change and improve what you do requires input focus on what is really important at that moment in time, together with the ability to be distracted less often. Focus is a learnt strength which, like all other strengths, requires effort and deliberate practice. It can in time lead to a state of 'Flow' which is an effortless state of performance in which you are completely absorbed in the task and lose track of time.

- **Feedback**—seek immediate feedback from whatever source is available. One of the most powerful and least used, is from our self. Become aware of what you did and how you did it then look for how effective it was. It could be as simple as a word you used, a smile, staying with a thought a little bit longer. Learn from every experience. We are designed to do this. Unfortunately most of us do not learn how to focus. What we often do is avoid the activity that did not work as planned. Get feedback and use it productively.

With an increase in awareness in real time, we can develop other new strengths that are needed to perform even better. Performance increases by reducing those activities that do not add value and increasing those that do.

It really is that simply. How we do it is through action based natural learning.

CHAPTER 4

Natural Learning

Quote: 'Learning is physical. Learning means the modification, growth, and pruning of our neurons, connections—called synapses—and neuronal networks; through experience . . . we are cultivating our own neuronal networks.' Dr. James Zull, Professor of Biology and Biochemistry at Case Western University, Ohio

Dr Zull is not referring to our hard wired neural pathways but to the new soft neural wired links generated through experience. These are created throughout our lives if we use our mind.

Learning

What more can be said about learning? It has been a major feature of most of our lives from a very early age. We attended school, college and, for some, university. We are imbued with knowledge in ever widening subjects. At work, we are provided with more knowledge. Today we can seek knowledge on the World Wide Web. But are we really any wiser? Why do we still have major issues within organisations such as performance, communication, team working and leadership? Why do a lot of people resist change? What stops people taking action to change when it is so obviously the right thing to do?

The role of training at work is to provide a learning process that involves the acquisition of knowledge, sharpening of skills, concepts and rules. But does it work?

The reality is the transference of certain types of training back into the workplace is poor. This is probably why a lot of training providers are struggling to find work in the current climate of minimal or virtually no growth.

I am not anti-training. Before I go into detail I need to make it very clear what type of training I am referring too. Any training that has job specific requirement, for example, IT knowledge, health and safety, project management processes or technical knowledge does not fall into the category of ineffective training. In fact, the transference of these subjects back to the workplace is relatively high, if used. The topics of training where transference is poor include personal effectiveness, leadership, teams, motivation, time management, change, assertiveness, stress management and any subject that is often described as soft skills training.

The elephant in the room

A majority of soft skills training does not transfer easily back into the workplace. Research supports this claim. My own enquires suggests that the transfer rate is between 0% and 20%, whilst an academic in knowledge based training informed me at the beginning of 2012 that it was nearer 10% to 12%. People acquire the knowledge but not necessarily the know-how or have the will to implement it. How often has it happened to you?

A simple test I sometimes apply in a Mind Fit workshop is to ask participants if they have time pressures at work. Most hands go up. The next question is to ask if they have attended a time management programme. A similar number of hands usually go up. Being Knowledge Fit is important but only if that knowledge is relevant, accurate and useable. If not, it is wasting everyone's time, effort and money.

How often have we heard about or experienced people returning from training courses full of ideas, to very quickly lose the initiative or motivation as they knuckle down to work? They quickly end up doing what they have always done in the same way that they have always done it.

How is training measured?

In 1959 Donald Kirkpatrick published his four levels of training evaluation. They are:

1. Reaction of participant—what they thought and felt about the training.

2. Learning—the resulting increase in knowledge and/or capability.

3. Behaviour—extent of behaviour and capability improvement and implementation/ application.

4. Results—the effects on the business or environment resulting from the trainee's performance.

Later JJ Philips added a fifth level. This addition was that the return-on-investment should be included. The assumption is that all of those methods for measuring training are linked. This proved not to be true.

Unfortunately, most training organisations only measure Kirkpatrick number 1 in the form of 'happy sheets' and occasionally, Kirkpatrick's number 2. Very few measure 3 or 4.

During the 1980s concern was growing over the limited impact soft training was having in the 'real' world of work. Following research by Alliger and Janak (1989) it was identified that the correlation between the four Kirkpatrick stages was not much better than chance. In other words, knowing about theories and concepts that supposedly affect the bottom line may not actually be related to work at all in a useable way. The input may be interesting but so what? That is not why organisations send people on programmes unless it is for personal development. The Chartered Institute of Personnel and Development (CIPD) published a report in 2007 and reinforced this again in 2009, which referred to Alliger and Janak, said that the transfer of knowledge into action is random chance.

Although the direct evidence may be limited because of the lack of measuring and evaluating, particularly on Kirkpatrick's levels 3 and 4, I would argue that there is evidence to show that a significant amount of training is not working. Many professional bodies have attempted to tackle these major issues at work that I referred to earlier that impact on performance and productivity. They include stress, absenteeism, conflict, disengagement and poor performance itself. Trainers have been delivering programmes to address these issues for years yet the reality is that they are either not working or only work to a small degree.

Let's remind ourselves some cost of these issues that still impact on performance. In 2006 the cost of training in the UK was put at £33.3 billion (Personnel Today). In June 2010 the Confederation of Business Industry (CBI) put the cost of absenteeism at £17 billion. The CIPD put the cost of conflict at £24 billion. In 2008 Gallup put the cost of disengagement between £59 billion to £64 billion and other sources have put the cost of poor performance at £70 billion. Disengagement is a real issue as it is linked to the other problems. The level of passively and actively disengaged people at work in the UK is between 70% and 80%. Similar levels of disengagement are found in all major economies around the world.

These are very scary figures that have a huge negative impact on the economy of the UK and other countries. They clearly indicate that training is not working as well as it should because it is not addressing the fundamental issues, even though training providers purport that it does. It is not knowledge that performs, it is people taking action. And, as we will discover later in this book, people come with a very complex array of beliefs, ideas, attitudes and behaviours which undoubtedly influence their performance. Many of those beliefs are based on a 'can't do' or 'won't do' attitude which is where disengagement sits.

If a significant level of non technical training is poor at transferring the learning back into the workplace, we need to ask why? Could it be that we have known about it for years and done nothing about it? This may explain why certain forms of training are one of the first things to go during periods of economic turmoil.

One possible reason for the failure of soft skilled knowledge based training to transfer into the workplace is that providing people with a range of theories and concepts is only ever going to be interesting. Examples such as Maslow, Hertzberg and Vroom on motivation or theories which compare situational, transactional and transformational leadership are useful if studying for example, a degree. Providing this type of knowledge is similar to teaching a person learning to drive a car the mechanical elements of what makes a car move in different directions and speed up. Interesting for some but not necessary to know when learning to drive a car.

I recently attended a training programme on the mindset of people relating to health and safety at work. The trainer said at the beginning of the day that his job was to impart knowledge to the participants. He said that whether people use that knowledge is down to them. I disagree. A trainer should take responsibility, directly or indirectly, for ensuring that people do take action back at work. It should also be measured against the business needs. If not, then the training has been a waste of everyone's time. We can no longer leave it to random chance.

As I have said, the world is changing at an unprecedented rate and at a time of the greatest uncertainty most of us have ever experienced. If training has not worked to the level it should in the good times, it is time to try a different approach now the times are tough. Part of the Mind Fit approach is aimed at changing beliefs, attitudes and behaviours first before giving people the relevant and useable knowledge that they need to do the job.

What difference would it make to performance if significantly more people started their journey with a 'can do' attitude and were engaged at work?

Some people do change

Of course, a small number of people do become more productive after attending personal development programmes, but, as we know, such people are quite rare. Interestingly, my work looking at why training was not having the impact it should found that the content and quality of most training programmes was virtually irrelevant. These 'can do' people were going to change anyway, and took whatever 'gems' they could from every learning opportunity. I needed to understand what makes these people tick.

Fourteen years ago I started interviewing people from organisations in both public and private sectors. I concluded that real change to perform came from those people who have an open, agile, positive and flexible mindset. A 'can do' mindset. These people had learnt and developed the capacity to handle the complexity of different situations in a productive manner and to take other people with them.

Today, I call such people Mind Fit. This is the prerequisite state to increasing performance and productivity whether as an individual, leader or team player.

Mind Fitness and learning

To generate lasting behavioural change, a person has to change the way they think, how they manage their feelings, and to have greater insights into their beliefs, values and attitudes. In addition, how they relate to other people. To achieve such deep, personal change we need to understand the nature of the learning which created the person in the first place. The type of learning used to develop Mind Fitness is as different from educated learning as chalk is to cheese. Psychologists call it implicit learning. I call it natural learning. Natural learning occurs mainly at an unconscious level as it is automatic. Most of us are largely unaware such learning is happening.

Simply put, we learn naturally about the world and ourself organically and instinctively. Of course, most people's internal mindset and external behaviours become a range of habits, some good and others not. This unwitting learning of who we are and what to do sits at the heart of learning to have a 'can't do', 'won't do' or 'can do' attitude. The following diagram offers a simple way to understand the differences between natural and educational learning.

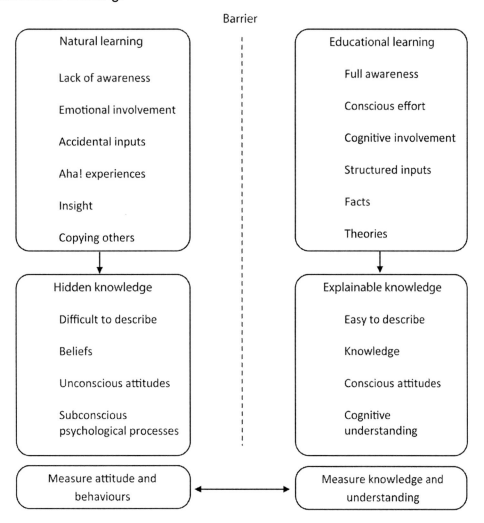

A simple example of the application of natural learning is tying a shoelace. You learn by being shown, copying and practicing until you succeed. You believe that you can do it so you persevere until you are successful. Now try describing to someone how to tie a shoelace. It is surprisingly difficult.

Natural learning

All people are born with the innate potential to be Mind Fit and healthy. Babies are naturally curious, inquisitive and fearless in their search for new information and knowledge. As life goes on, however, outside factors begin to have an effect. Absent or unsupportive parents, unkind or overstretched teachers, bad experiences in the playground and later the workplace all take their toll. And this effect can take the form of a negative, helpless or defensive approach to life. In short, a lack of Mind Fitness is a learned rather than innate behaviour. We can all choose to learn to become more Mind Fit, with a 'can do' attitude—or mind UN-Fit, perhaps with a cynical, negative attitude to life.

Good habits and bad habits

Some people instinctively learn good psychological habits that help them to feel Mind Fit and in control. This gives them a sense of Personal Power. These are the ones that always take something away from a training input. They have real confidence, a 'can do' attitude and the ability to engage and inspire others. They make great leaders, great team members—and great parents.

The problem is that we can also learn bad habits which can have a negative effect on both our mind and bodies—and this learning is also just as effortless. It can lead to people developing 'can't do' attitudes. Such people may become insecure, have a sense of being overwhelmed and lack confidence. Martin Seligman, guru of positive psychology, described this state as Learned Helplessness. The 'won't do' people, those who have learnt to be defensive, also operate from a dysfunctional state. They may exhibit cynical or perfectionist attitudes and behaviours. They tend to blame others, may become bullies or be just plain awkward. I call this Learned Defensiveness®. Inside, such people have a sense of being vulnerable and have a deep need to protect themselves.

The Personal Profile Map® is a simple diagram showing the three distinct characteristics on three continuums.

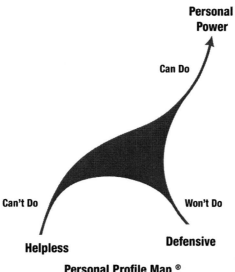

Personal Profile Map ®

Important reminder

Natural learning occurs automatically, often without us being aware of it. It provides us not only with many of our skills and abilities but with the means to make sense of our world and how to operate in it. For some people, it is about surviving, for others, how to thrive and grow.

Here are some ways we learn naturally:

- **Maps**—people need maps, accurate or not, to help them understand where they are and where they are going in all different scenarios. We construct many maps on how to behave in different situations. This may be at a networking event, social function, business meeting and so on. The Personal Profile Map® which you will get to know throughout this book is a constructed map of three core ways that people tend to operate.

- **Physical experiences**—we learn by doing. Sometimes by accident or mistake. By taking deliberate action we can become very aware of what is happening and learn from the experience. Even a simple thing like learning to text with your thumb is an example of how quickly we can learn naturally if we apply our self. If we don't, we won't.

- **Learning from others**—we observe and we copy. We assimilate and replicate. Being given an opportunity to shadow someone at work can be immensely important. Also we learn by observing bad behaviours. I was once approached by a very senior person in the organisation whilst I was in the company of my team leader. The senior person asked my colleague who I was. I started to answer and was promptly told by the senior person that he does not talk to people from the shop floor. I learnt not to replicate that sort of behaviour because it made me feel angry and that is not good for relationships.

- **Mind experiences**—some include using our imagination. Others can be instant, such as those 'light bulb' moments. Light bulb moments come when we are thinking, trying to make sense of something. Some appear fast whilst others evolve. The key is to think.

- **Stories**—we all remember good stories, and the lessons endure. Many go back to our childhood. People often remember stories much easier than theories or data.

- **Comments and feedback**—these can be either powerful or destructive. So many of us avoid comments or feedback because we fear being 'criticised' and that is not pleasant. The more Mind Fit you become, the more you will actively seek feedback because that enables you to learn and move forward.

- **Passion**—to improve, to grow, to be successful in your chosen topic. It provides so much positive energy rather than the apathy or cynicism that can permeate where passion is not evident.

All of these ways of learning naturally can have both a positive and negative impact. Learn from both.

The key is to take control of natural learning and use it. Direct focused effort on those small inputs within each challenge will build success. Mind Fitness is increased through focused effort, perseverance and feedback.

Target this focused effort on increasing your own and your team's personal and business performance. In the process you will enhance your Mind Fitness.

The change journey

The good news is that people do not start out life as being helpless or defensive. They have learnt it naturally which means that those dysfunctional attitudes, behaviours and habits can be changed in the same natural way that lead to more positive ones.

Mind Fitness using action based natural learning is the process to achieve this. This is obvious when you consider how we learn to swim, drive a car, present to an audience or engage customers. Knowing about the subject may have some benefit but the real learning comes from doing.

Knowledge training is not a waste of time

Once again it is important to emphasise that relevant knowledge which is useable is an important part of a much wider picture. The danger is when it is considered sufficient on its own. Clearly, it is not, and it is by linking appropriate knowledge based training with Mind Fitness that participants develop their sense of Personal Power.

Mind Fit people are able to operate effectively in today's economic turmoil because they are in personal control and take action. We need more people like them who are active. People who put the effort in, in a deliberate focused way. What difference would it make to you, your business or team if more of your people were Mind Fit?

Of course, an essential element of Mind Fitness development and using natural learning is having a 'can do' belief. So many of our beliefs actually block us from taking action. Why?

CHAPTER 5

Beliefs

Quote: 'Human beings, by changing the (**inner beliefs**) of their mind, can change the outer aspects of their lives.' Williams James c1890

In the preface I made reference to beliefs by saying that one of the biggest obstacles to discovering something new is the belief that we already know it. This is so true. The assumption that we already know something invariably stops us from thinking. An ability to think flexibly is one of the core components of Mind Fitness and enhanced performance.

As I alluded to in the previous chapter, many of our beliefs also stop us from taking action. We may believe that we are not very good at public speaking, or someone is better at analysing detail or at grammar than we are, so we do not try. We may believe that we are not creative and therefore do not use our imagination or we believe that we are naturally shy so we avoid social events.

So what are beliefs? How important are they?

First, beliefs have nothing to do with reality. They are something that we have accepted as a truth and built it into our own inner reality as a truth. They are buried in our deep non-thinking self. Accepting something as true without thinking it through appears to be part of our human make up. Think about some of the items of news we read in the daily papers. How often do we accept the headlines as facts?

Unfortunately, not all beliefs are positive. Some are negative; they can have a mixed impact on our mind and behaviour. This is why some people often avoid taking action because they believe they are not capable of doing whatever is needed. They have made themselves mind UN-Fit through a belief and by reinforcing that belief through natural learning.

So what we believe is what we see. Not the other way round.

Beliefs and reality

A former research psychologist I worked with told me that theories are not truths but in every theory there is a truth. Theories are tested over and over again by very dedicated people with the purpose of affirming or destroying the theory. Many of these theories become adopted by lay people or some trainers as a truth even though they have only read or understood the headlines. Some theories become obsolete as new ones take their place yet many old ones persist and impact on how we think and what we do.

There are many people who still believe that our personality is fixed in our DNA and we are what we are, we cannot change them; that our genes drive our behaviour, which is why we cannot help ourself sometimes. It creates a 'not my fault mentality'. Or that some people are born with innate talents. Such beliefs make us the victim of our hereditary. What do you believe? If you believe you cannot change you will not.

There is growing evidence from the world of biology, neuroscience and epigenetic that our personality can be changed, if we choose to change it. That our genes only partially drive us but we mainly respond to the environment, real or perceived, which switches on our genes. And people are not born with innate talents but innate assets and those that become peak performers spend years dedicated to focused practice on their chosen sport, hobby or interest. But do not believe me. Look at the research evidence. Challenge your own beliefs.

What is good news is that we can control our beliefs, our personal environment and how we think. We can choose to change.

None of us are born with beliefs. A great many are acquired before adulthood from those closest to us, whilst others will become part of our being as we experience various life challenges. As the Jesuits have stated, 'Give me a boy up to seven and I will give you the man'. They knew that at a very young age, our imaginative and fertile mind, absorbed information at an incredible rate and the information given to us, becomes undisputable fact. Religious beliefs testify to this. At that young age we do not have the capability to rationalise or analyse what we are told. We just accept it as true. Why not? We trust our parents, relatives, teachers and spiritual leaders.

The Jesuits considered it was important to give a child information early because we absorb more when young. Today, we know the process of absorbing information never stops.

How many of us still have recall to that early learning on how to behave today? Are any of you affected by some early 'instructions' given to us by our parents, those closest to us and teachers such as:

- Be perfect

- Be strong

- Try hard

- Please people

- Hurry up

Or sweeping statements like:

- "I MUST finish this piece of work, and I MUST do it perfectly."

- "I MUST be popular with everyone".

- "I MUST be good at everything and MUST never make mistakes".

- "It would be absolutely totally AWFUL if I get shouted at, or if my friend doesn't call back tonight".

Beliefs about ourself, others, the world and how we operate in it have profound, powerful and pervasive effects on individuals. They are sometimes difficult to be aware of, and can sometimes clash with other people's belief systems, causing interpersonal difficulties.

All are buried deep within our subconscious mind and often only surface when we are confronted with a challenge or issue. We use these beliefs to construct our own reality. Many are unique to us and some we may share. These personal belief constructs give meaning to various aspects of our lives which enable us to make sense of our world by constructing our own reality.

Constructs

What is a construct? When we consider what a construct is we quickly realise that a majority of our understanding of how we operate is made up of constructs. Some constructs are formed by beliefs as found in various religions across the world. Others have a scientific backdrop to them. Some could be a mixture of fact or fiction.

The weather is a construct. The weather does not exist as a fact in scientific terms. It is made up of various measureable facts or components such as temperature, air pressure, humidity and wind speed. By analysing the components we can construct and describe the 'weather'. And when we hear a weather forecast we all have a shared understanding what the forecaster is describing.

Other constructs include motivation, communication, thinking, values and performance. Small components of these words when put together, often at a subconscious level, provide us with an understanding of what we mean by each of those constructs. Of course, my understanding of values or motivation could be different from yours. So who is right?

Let's consider motivation. To be more motivated we need to know what the small components are that make up motivation. Without them, motivation is just a word which sounds important but lacks the detail we need to take action. That in turn makes it virtually impossible to know what and how to change. Identify those components that make up motivation then we have something to work with.

At a personal level at work we might be motivated by money, being told what to do, by the security the job provides, the rewards we receive or the threat of losing a promotion. We could also be motivated by having a meaningful sense of purpose as with a nurse or a teacher. It may meet social needs or the job may provide learning opportunities. We might be motivated by being given responsibility or to handle new projects. Motivators are usually very personal and deeply held which is why many motivation theories on their own lack the breadth of understanding.

By accepting that we all construct different realities then we can start to understand what makes us both complex and different. Not right or wrong but with a different perspective of our world and how we operate in it. Later, I will explain how we can use this complexity to construct our own Personal Profile Map® which we can all intuitively understand, and share that understanding.

Fact or fiction

Over the years I have noticed how easily all of us pick up beliefs, which form our unique constructs, without querying them. We read a snippet of information or hear something on the television. A friend at work passes on a rumour they have heard. All become 'facts' in our mind. We do not ask the questions, 'What is the source?' 'How reliable is it?' 'Where is the evidence?'

Here are two examples.

I was recently invited to attend a workshop on emotional intelligence. I sat throughout the day and listened to the trainer, who informed us about the 'science' behind the programme whilst making links to different aspects of our emotions and its impact in the world of work and relationships. The group consisted of HR professionals, trainers and coaches. The trainer talked to us for six hours, during which he reinforced what he had said with words on PowerPoint slides and in the workbook provided.

At the end of the day he informed us that effective communication is 55% body language, 38% tone of voice and 7% the words we used. I had heard this many times before and I am always intrigued by how readily people accept this as a truth. No one queried it. They treated the information as a scientific fact. The group went on to discuss this amazing piece of science as a reality.

What is the reality? Well, common sense tells us if 93% of effective communication is based on body language and tone of voice, why do we waste time with words? Why not mime and make noises like whales and dolphins. Learning a foreign language would be simple as we would not have to learn words or the complexity of grammar.

The research on effective communication which the trainer was referring to, like so many others, was taken out of context so that the wrong conclusions were drawn. The original research was conducted in 1971 by Professor Albert Mehrabian who concluded that body language, tone of voice and words are the basic elements of face-to-face communication. No surprise there.

The percentages so often quoted are based on a second piece of the research. Whether or not you like or dislike a person. Imagine for whatever reason you have decided that you dislike someone. Whatever they say the probability is that you will not hear the words. Their body language and tone of voice will dominate. You will have made your mind up.

Other factors also come into play when communicating. For example; our feelings, values, meanings, beliefs and attitude also have to be taken in to the equation. In reality, communication is more complex than a commonly quoted set of percentages.

A second myth which continually resists reality relates to talents. Organisations seek out innate talent at work, use tests for talent and use language that reinforces the belief that some people are naturally talented. Talents are linked to our personal strengths and there is a huge strength industry where organisations can identify the main strengths that you use. Playing to our strengths seems the obvious thing to do. Why waste time on weaknesses?

But are talents and strengths innate? The simple answer is no. If you do not believe me look up the research by K Anders Ericsson, Professor of Psychology at Florida State University. And he is not the only scientist with this view formed from years of research.

He states, 'the traditional assumption is that people come into a professional domain, have similar experiences, and the only thing that's different is their innate abilities. There's little evidence to support this. With the exception of some sports, no characteristic of the brain or body constrains an individual from reaching an expert level. What does constrain them are personal beliefs.'

Unfortunately, the talent and strength industry plays to the belief.

Innate assets

We are all born with innate assets not talents, but most of us do not use them. For example, we are all born to be long distance runners. Our anatomy and our skeletal muscles are designed to enable us to run over very long distances, which is why our ancestors survived and we are here today. How many of us become long distance runners? Very few.

We have an innate ability to make variable sounds. We then learn naturally to turn that innate ability into a language by copying others and practicing.

Our innate assets enable us to be creative, innovative and potentially entrepreneurial. Our brain structure contains a large component which enables us to use our imagination to look back on past events or create different futures. Yet early experiences, those closest to us and our education system, leave many of us believing otherwise.

An academic who was participating in a Mind Fit workshop stated that he was told at school that he was no good at art, in particular painting. He said that he did not paint again for 30 years. Recently he decided to try it again and discovered that he is actually very good. It just took focused effort and perseverance.

Becoming a top golfer, racing driver, sales person or leader is not the result of innate talents or personal strengths. It is to do with something that we all have the ability to do. So what makes someone good at what they do and for a few, exceptionally great? The simple answer is focused effort and perseverance. The more you practice the better you get so long as what you practice is focused on the input. Research evidence over many years shows that to become an 'expert' you have to commit about 10,000 focused hours to your chosen topic or sport, which normally takes place over ten years.

To become great at a particular sport or playing a musical instrument, an early start in life is essential but in other spheres that is not the case. We discover all through our lives that we can become good or even great at something if we are interested and persevere at the chosen subject. Not only does this relate to personal interests but includes leadership, project management, public speaking and so on. Given the opportunity and drive it is amazing what people can achieve.

Charles Darwin, who revolutionised our understanding of human evolution, showed no particular drive to learn and discover as a young man. He was a complete disappointment to his parents. He was more interested in shooting and dogs. Thomas Edison, the great inventor was expelled from school because his teacher thought him 'retarded'. Albert Einstein started out life as a patent clerk and showed no particular 'talents' yet went on to become one of the greatest physicists ever.

For most of us at work, we only need to be effective, not exceptional and the hours we need to commit to becoming an effective performer is actually very few. What generally gets in the way is the belief that we can't do something, or someone else is better, or it is not my job. Many people at work spend a lot of time procrastinating or prevaricating, and not focused on what they should be doing.

Beliefs and direction

Hopefully by now you will recognise that our behaviour and corresponding performance is often based on beliefs we have constructed about our self, others and the world we operate in. Those beliefs become embedded into our reality and consistently impact on our decision making.

Neuroscience today is informing us that upto 95% of the decisions we make are made unconsciously and automatically. Many of those decisions will be biased towards negativity and paralysis. Unfortunately, this negative type of thinking can dominate many people's lives rendering them mind UN-Fit. Such beliefs develop dominating 'can't do' or 'won't do' attitudes. Those attitudes in turn impact on how we behave.

Reflect on the speed you make decisions. How many are virtually instinctive? How many are thought through?

Consider a challenge that you have faced recently. What did you believe about it and your ability to tackle it? Which route did you take on the diagram below?

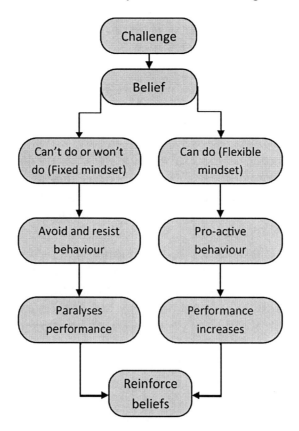

How often do you put off or avoid doing what you need to do? It may be you avoid picking up the telephone to make that important call or fail to deal with conflict or underperformance in your team. What are the beliefs behind these failures to act?

A simple test

If you are asked to juggle with three balls what is your immediate response? Is it can't or can do?

When presenting, I regularly ask people to come out and juggle. I hold three juggling balls in my hand offering them to the group or audience. For the great majority the response is a simple 'I can't juggle'. Others avoid eye contact whilst some seek to justify their unwillingness to participate by saying 'I've tried and failed so I know I can't juggle'. A few say 'Why should I. There is no benefit'. The latter point is well made; however, sitting behind the comment is 'I can't'.

What core strengths do you need to be able to juggle? Hand and eye co-ordination and a sense of physical power, an image of juggling and the strength to persevere. The number of personal strengths is actually very few. What you do need is a belief you can juggle with focused effort and practice.

My next question is 'Can you drive a car?' The great majority say yes. What strengths do you need to drive a car? You have undoubtedly realised where I am going with this. Driving a car is far more complex than juggling. You need hand, eye and foot co-ordination, spatial awareness, foresight, the ability to analyse information rapidly, quick problem solving abilities and emotional control. I do acknowledge that we may vary in these strengths but we do all possess them.

It is much harder to drive a car than to juggle three balls.

Of course, for most of us there are many more benefits in our society to driving a car than juggling. A Mind Fit person, and I come across many, when faced with the question about juggling may answer something like this. 'I can juggle but not very well. Maybe with two balls at the moment. If I practice I will be able to improve my juggling. However, I choose not to because there is no benefit'. This response is based on thinking, challenging internal beliefs and making an informed decision.

What would be the benefit for you at work if you learnt to respond in a Mind Fit way to the challenges and opportunities that occur?

The power of beliefs

Acknowledging that beliefs can cause a lack of reasoned thinking resulting in inactivity is a start point. The following example of a strongly held belief emphasises how you can challenge them.

This organisation was responsible for handling parking and other traffic related tickets on behalf of a local authority. They were failing. The tickets had to be processed within six months of the event to comply with the law. After which they were out of time for a prosecution. The organisation had a backlog of over 5000 tickets which they were unable to process which meant that the legal time elapsed for action on them and the local authority lost revenue. This was an ongoing problem.

The manager was suffering from stress caused by a very strong belief that the problem could not be solved. This belief had been reinforced by her direct manager who declined to support her and told her that she could not have any additional resources. He also told her it was her job, not his, to come up with a solution: a not untypical response that many of us have been faced with.

The manager came to me for help. She joined a group and took part in a day focused on how to become Mind Fit. She identified those strengths she needed to do her job well. On the second day the focus moved to solving work related problems. But now the manager had a different mindset: a 'can do' one.

She thought through the problem, identified what she had to do to conform to the law and came up with some innovative solutions. She felt confident enough to take some calculated risks that would lead to solving the problem. She decided to employ three temporary staff and in consultation with her team, she simplified the process, in some cases by challenging old engrained policies and procedures. She brought in flexible working hours, which enabled the limited office space to be used to its maximum. She consulted with legal advisors. She took focused action.

A problem which seemed unsolvable was resolved in seven weeks and over £300,000 was recovered for the local authority. The start point that led to the successful outcome was to become Mind Fit. During the journey, which took place over a day, the manager identified and challenged her negative beliefs. Next day she adopted a completely different mindset. She conducted a reality check against her beliefs, identified areas where actions could be implemented and left with a plan. She involved her staff in the process and they took an action focused approach.

Changing beliefs

Take a look at the checkerboard below. The reality is the squares with the 'A' and 'B' on, are the same shade. This is a fact. But do you believe this bold statement because the squares with the letters on look different shades?

Edward H. Adelson

If you do not believe me look up Edward H Adelson's light perception experiments on the web. They are fascinating. Believing is seeing. If you believe something is true, then it is true for you. As Henry Ford said, 'If you believe you can or you believe you can't, you are right'.

Changing beliefs requires an awareness of the belief.

- **Awareness**—this is once again a major strength that is critical here. Identifying our own beliefs, both positive and those that sabotage our thinking can only be achieved if we know what they are and how they impact on what we do. We can then choose to change them. Awareness is one of the major strengths that people have consistently told us over the years that enabled them to take personal control and move forward.

- **Beliefs**—identify your personal beliefs as often as you can. Become aware of what you are thinking, that internal dialogue that goes on within your mind all the time. The beliefs are there all the time because they form our internal map of how we operate, but most of us are not aware of them. Identify the positive beliefs, the negative ones and those that do not matter either way. For example, the latter could relate a model of car you believe is better than another one. Some people believe that a Mercedes car is better than a BMW whilst others have the opposite view. Try and change that particular belief. If the beliefs have no meaningful impact, leave them. Decide which beliefs you need to change because they are destructive.

- **Challenge**—seek out the evidence that supports your belief. Make sure that what you believe does not result in what you see. We can all be blind if we want to. Ask people, search the Web, read books and think. If the belief is not constructive, change it.

- **Stop**—stop doing those things that sabotage you. Simply replace old negative beliefs and habits with new positive ones. It is in your control.

By challenging and taking control of our beliefs we can control our thinking, feelings and drivers. We can give ourself choices about how we live our lives and tackle the situations that confront us. We can become 'can do' people and if we choose to, innovative and entreprenurial.

Finally, as you will be recognising, with our different understanding of what makes us what we are, how we learn and the power of personal beliefs and constructs, we are all very complex, yet there is a pattern to our complexity which we need to explore next. Thankfully, this complexity does form easily recognisable patterns and trends.

CHAPTER 6

Complex Adaptive Systems

Quote: 'A complex system that works is invariably found to have evolved from a simple system that worked. A complex system designed from scratch never works and cannot be patched up to make it work. You have to start over, beginning with a working simple system.' John Gall

This was my challenge. To make the complex simple, easily understood and intuitively right.

For years science saw the world and people as linear systems where everything, once understood, was logical, explainable and controllable. Its core has thinking based on linear systems models that have a cause and effect view. A mechanistic world where order could be achieved once you understood the parts and the relationship to and between each part. Science today informs us that linear systems are rare.

Unfortunately, the majority of people and organisations have not realised that this is the case. Education is a linear system which people enter in yearly batches, often when reaching the age of five. Knowledge input is provided in silos: maths, language, science. The system has become dominant in our early development and has often lost any meaningful link with other facets of life, such as work.

Many of these educational processes are moving further and further away from the other perceived linear system that education should be supporting: work. The pursuit of a curriculum controlled by central government in the UK, obsessed with testing and higher education, has led to many young people entering the world of work without any understanding of the real complexity that they face or of the world of work.

To make matters worse, if you are labelled as having learning difficulties such as dyslexia, then you are moved further away from being prepared for work. I have met many dyslexics who do not try because they believe that they 'cannot do'. The system and the label they have been given verifies this and rendered them helpless and a feeling of being useless. Dyslexics just learn differently, albeit in a more chaotic or innovative way, but they can learn. And dyslexics can be very effective and productive as two well known apparent dyslexics have shown: Albert Einstein and Richard Branson.

Organisations are no better when it comes to linear systems. Structures are created, lines of communications are drawn, linear processes are developed and people parts are put into place where they are deemed necessary. In reality, some linear systems can work to some degree as in 'lean' management. However, people operate the systems and people are definitely not a linear construct. As I have already mentioned, even in the ultimate lean process developed and used by a Japanese car manufacturer, things went wrong which caused a massive financial loss and, more importantly, a loss to customer confidence.

To make matters worse, some of this linear thinking is directly related to people at work. Organisations create business strategies, logical plans which at some point are linked to individuals often through HR practices and training. The expectation is that this will lead to people behaving in a predictable way so that the plan will be met, productivity increased and targets achieved. Take this example of linear thinking by a sales manager who told his sales team that if they make 100 telephone calls they should get 10 appointments which will lead to one new client. It appeared to him to be blindingly obvious. Unfortunately, people are involved and they are unpredictable. His expected results failed to materialise.

We are still consumed in our day to day world with the belief that if certain things are put into place in a set order, then predictable results will follow. Many business consultants fall into this trap. How misguided we are with this completely wrong thinking because the nature of the beast is unpredictability. The world post 2007 is definitely more complex.

The leather factory

I came across this when a leather manufacturer merged two factories. The belief was the output would remain the same and that a reduction in costs could be achieved. Output of 100 tons of processed leather from one factory plus 50 tons from a second factory would lead to 150 tons. When the figures came in the total production was consistently around 132 tons. What caused the loss were the people. The directors had failed to acknowledge that people are not that simple. They are complex and did not do what was logically expected. These were the people who kept moving the items around in circles so it created an illusion of efficiency because it stopped management from chasing them up.

We all know that the reality is somewhat different from what is predicted on spreadsheets. People do not operate as predictable linear systems, neither do organisations nor the processes within. We are surrounded by the evidence. Underperformance is rife, conflicts common, disengagement is hitting nearly 80%, stress remains high and sales results are varied.

What can we do?

It is time to accept that we all exist in a very complex world made more uncertain by the current economic climate which is totally unpredictable.

The good news is that although people are very complex, there are patterns to how we all function which are to a degree predictable and which once we are made aware of them, we can take significant control of ourself and what we do.

The patterns that lead to Mind Fitness or mind UN-Fitness

Let me remind you that effective Mind Fitness is composed of four core parts of our mind. They are:

- **Thinking self**—The ability to think flexible and focus appropriately.

- **Feeling self**—Being emotionally competent and resilient.

- **Driving self**—Committed with a real sense of purpose.

- **Social self**—Being able to connect meaningfully with others.

The positive combination of these four parts helps us predetermine to some degree the attitudes and behaviours which forms the Personal Power section of the Personal Profile Map® shown on the next page. Someone who is Mind Fit will operate from a position of Personal Power. They will have the confidence, drive, courage and resilience needed to handle their own complexity and that of the world they exist in.

Conversely, someone who is mind UN-Fit, will feel very insecure about how to handle the moment and their future. Some people may have the knowledge but have a rigid and closed mindset rendering them mind UN-Fit. They will avoid facing new challenges and blame everyone else when things go wrong.

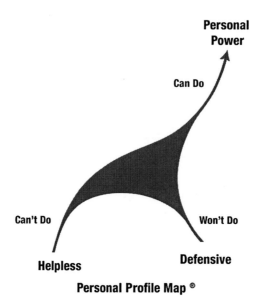

Personal Profile Map ®

In reality, we can learn to consistently operate in any of the three extremes shown on the map. An event can also move us up or down the map, as many people would have discovered recently if faced with the prospect of redundancy from work. I have met those that see it as the end of their working life whilst others see it as a new beginning.

The pattern, which eventually leads to Mind Fitness and Personal Power, is constructed from numerous strengths and weaknesses developed by each of us over years. Each can be connected in an unpredictable way as indicated in the diagram below. Many of these connections form, what is often generally referred to in our daily lives, as our character or personality.

This diagram shows a sample of strengths and weaknesses with a few connections. There will be many more. As these connections cluster, they start to form patterns of attitudes and behaviours.

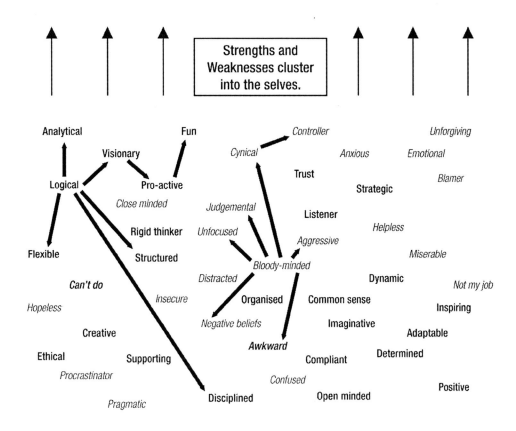

We can cluster those random words into patterns that directly link to our four selves: how we think, feel, those drivers and relationships.

The next diagram simply suggests the patterns that can be formed and placed into the four selves.

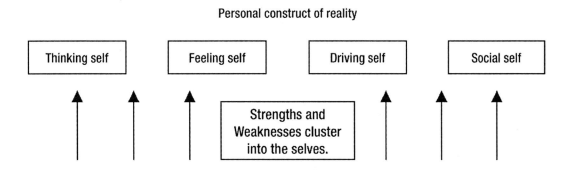

This in turn forms our unique and personal construct. For example, the descriptive word 'supportive' can be linked to strengths such as empathy, to listening, to accepting. All fit into the social self and are part of how we connect meaningfully with others. Conversely, visionary, detailed and organised will form part of how we think. I have placed these strengths with others in the four selves below. There will be many more which we have developed.

Mind Fit four selves			
Thinking self	**Feeling self**	**Driving self**	**Social self**
Ability to think flexibly and appropriately	*Emotionally competent and resilient*	*Committed with a real sense of purpose*	*Connect meaningfully with others*
• Visionary	• Enthusiastic	• Can do beliefs	• Accepting
• Detailed	• Energetic	• Determined	• Supportive
• Organised	• Calm	• Loyal	• Listening

Of course, it is not all positive as the four selves are also applicable to helpless and defensive states. 'Can't do', insecurity and compliant are weaknesses and form part of our driving self, albeit from a helpless perspective. Whilst cynical, blame focused and obstructive is a defensive cluster. These become blockers instead of drivers.

By clustering Mind Fit strengths and mind UN-Fit weaknesses forms the basis of how we operate in different situations. These strengths and weaknesses have evolved and changed continually throughout our lives.

The four selves are unique to developing Mind Fitness. This whole brain approach enables us to place our strengths, or if appropriate, weaknesses into each of the four selves. Now everyone of us can to choose to change by stopping a weakness and add whatever strength we decide would be beneficial to us. All it takes is focused effort and perseverance which are also strengths in their own right.

By doing this we are in a position to apply some control over what initially seems unpredictable from the myriad of strengths and weaknesses we all possess. As we will discover, unpredictability still remains at the core of complex adaptive systems, albeit we can make sense of it and use it.

Finally, our personal construct based on the four selves now leads to the Personal Profile Map® as three very distinct forms of attitudes and behaviours: 'can't do', 'won't do' and 'can do', emerge. By identifying your own strengths and weaknesses relating to your four selves you can plot them on to the Personal Profile Map® under whatever state they apply to. It provides you with a sense of direction from which you can choose to take action as desired.

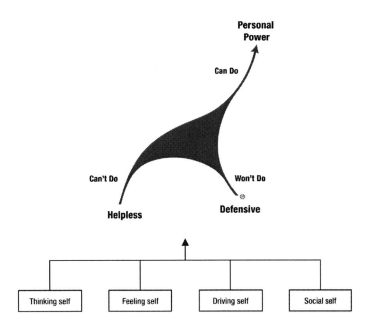

If you identify a weakness in your thinking self such as prevarication, you can simply acknowledge it and do something different like make the phone call or raise an issue with a colleague. Practice it and it will soon become a new habit.

Complex Adaptive Systems (CAS)

I have consistently referred to the complexity and unpredictability of all of us. Mind Fitness recognises and acknowledges this complexity. The work I undertook to construct the Personal Profile Map® built on our four selves, acknowledges that we are a complex adaptive system. What is missing from the Personal Profile Map® and its relationship to our four selves is the plethora of mutual connections between the strengths and weaknesses and how they can affect each other.

The reason I do not show them is that the connections made are unique to each and every one of us and will vary according to our own experiences, beliefs, changes in the environment and our thinking. Put this complexity into working relationships and to meeting business plans increases the challenge. Thankfully, because it is possible to predict some of the patterns, the Mind Fitness process works.

By adding a new strength and reducing a weakness the pattern will change. It will undoubtedly have an effect on all the selves. If you have a tendency not to listen, which is a weakness in the social self, and start to listen effectively, then it will improve not only the relationship but how you feel, how you think and maybe what you believe.

This is the very essence of developing Mind Fitness. As long as we are aware of what we are changing and why, then a small change can have a big impact.

The principles of a CAS

Understanding the rules of a complex adaptive system is helpful. We are surrounded by such systems and they have a huge impact on our lives. The current issues around the world economy and the Euro are the results of the unpredictability of two complex systems.

Complex adaptive systems have many properties. The most important in the field of Mind Fitness are the three principles of a complex adaptive system, relating in this case, to each and every one of us:

- The complex system's history is irreversible. It's happened.

- Order is emergent as opposed to predetermined. This is why business plans change.

- The complex system's future is unpredictable. Things always change.

This sounds remarkably like the psychology of most people and organisations particularly in the new world economy. Interestingly, the adaptations occur because the whole is made up from a number of discrete, but inter-relating components.

For the development of Mind Fitness these components relate to personal strengths and weaknesses. Each component is semi-autonomous yet can be linked and clustered to other components resulting in new emergent beliefs, attitudes and behaviours.

The way in which the components connect and relate to one another is critical as they ultimately, through patterns, lead to 'can't do', 'won't do' or 'can do' mindsets. Knowing this is important. It enables each of us to choose to break any connection by stop doing something and create another one with potentially, a more positive outcome. This, of course, is where there is some element of unpredictability.

Exactly what connections are made following a new action are once again unpredictable as there is no hierarchy and the connections are self-organising. This is why feedback is so important because it raises our level of awareness enabling us to take control and focus on what is important.

In any emerging patterns, simple rules often apply. If I smile at someone I will usually receive a positive response. If I moan at them I will possibly render their emotional state to one similar to mine. By placing this complexity into and on the Personal Profile Map® it gives us three very clear operating states:

- Helplessness—can't do and apathy

- Defensiveness—won't do and cynicism

- Powerful—can do and confidence

By relating everything we do back to the Personal Profile Map® we are provided with a simple but intuitively right model which we can use to understand and develop our own Mind Fitness and reduce those destructive mind UN-Fit elements.

The following map is a combination of the previous diagrams in this chapter. It links an unprecedented number of strengths and weaknesses in a random pattern which builds into our Personal Profile Map®.

Having a pattern means we can start to predict how and why we and other people react the way we do in different situations. Some are positive whilst others are negative. Being aware of this process enables all of us to place some control over the myriad of variable components and make those changes that we choose to, to improve the quality of our lives and achieve more at work.

Then we can construct a more beneficial way of living at work and in our personal lives.

Complexity into some form of order

The following map combines all layers of being human and why each of us is unique.

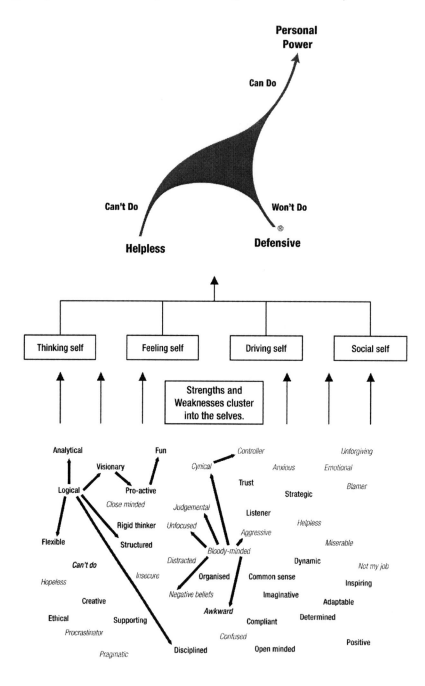

The good news is that each of us can choose which direction to travel on the Personal Profile Map®. Complex Systems are 'adaptable' so we can control them to a significant degree, albeit they still remain unpredictable. Using the simple pattern of the three key mindsets—'can't do', 'won't do' and 'can do' enables us to make choices.

Does having a pattern work? Look at it this way. Think of the complexity that must exist when a flock of starlings swerve and weave across the sky; it is an awe-inspiring display. If you are interested, look up 'Boids' on the web. It explains the simple 'rules' that are needed to create this display which prevents a disaster. These are my words but the rules are simple. Move more or less in the same direction at a similar speed, keep a set distance and don't crowd.

If one bird in the flock fails to follow these simple rules then chaos will occur. What happens in an organisation when one person refuses to conform to the collective and agreed way of working?

Becoming Mind Fit simply means tuning up this complex system by identifying some simple personal rules of engaging positively with the real world and other people in it. It really is as simple as that.

However, this can only happen if an individual is aware of the nature of the system, of the many possible ways that components interact, and finds ways to optimise their own system both within and between the four selves.

Because each of us is unique, with our own experience and not that of our genetic hereditary, we cannot predict what another individual needs to do to improve their Mind Fitness. It has to come from the individual. This is why the self assessment part of the process to becoming Mind Fit is essential. Individuals have to raise their level of awareness and self assess what they do, why they do it and the consequences of what they do. They can then relate this to their own Personal Profile Map® which they continue to build and change. This can then be collated into a team profile.

What does this mean in practice? Take someone who consistently focuses on the worst of everything or on those things that go wrong. A member of a local community, who was actively involved in helping the community achieve a reduction in the speed limit from 40mph to 30mph through his village, only ever 'saw' failure. The scheme was implemented and feedback came in from the community that the speed reduction was working. People felt less vulnerable when crossing the road or when entering or leaving their drives. Accidents were reduced. It was held by the community to be a great success.

Except for this one person who had been active in getting the speed reduction. One day, he watched two motorcyclists overtake cars outside of his property. The scheme as far as he is concerned, is an abject failure: waste of time, effort and money. He continues to moan about it to this day.

Should he choose to, all he needs to do is shift his focus from those occasional breaches of the law, which happen everywhere, to that of the great majority of drivers who conform. This shift in focus, with a bit of practice, would result in less anger, less stress and a sense of a job well done. Much healthier.

The Mind Fit process enables each individual to self assess and to choose what they need to stop doing and what they need to start doing.

What next?

For us, the whole of this Mind Fitness system is focused on achieving performance and success in the real world, whatever that might be. And in our workshop experience, we consistently find that when someone does make a small change in Mind Fitness, it does have a large impact—exactly as the non-linearity of a complex system would predict.

The Personal Profile Map® provides all of us with a constructed map that people have informed us is intuitively right. On this map, as people self assess, they can plot their own strengths and weaknesses which provide each individual with an indicator of what they need to stop doing and start doing to become Mind Fit.

Of course, understanding what strengths are and how they fit into our four selves is the next area to be explored. That will enable us to choose which strengths or weaknesses to work on.

CHAPTER 7

Strengths

Quote: 'No characteristic of the brain or body constrains an individual from reaching an expert level.' Dr. K. Anders Ericsson

In this chapter I challenge two perceived aspects of strengths that have a profound impact on how we operate personally and in many organisations. The first is the belief by many people, including many in positions of authority or power, that strengths are innate. Current research informs us otherwise. The second is that we should play to our strengths. This sounds obviously sensible; however, I will explain how this is a limiting view and that in today's difficult economic time we need to go beyond this. We need to unleash the best in everyone.

Strengths

For our purposes strengths are simply those things that we are good at, or, more importantly, those things we believe we are good at. Once again, beliefs are at the forefront of our strengths. However, we are about to enter a mine field because the origins of our personal strengths is still in debate. Are they innate or learnt?

A more formal definition of strengths, which I helped form is **'Strengths are empowering beliefs about our ability to utilise our innate psychological assets and employ effective learned personal strategies which together, contribute to our psychological capacity to perform'**. This definition suggests that we all have the assets within us. Unfortunately for many we do not believe it and therefore, do not apply those assets.

We are all born with the potential to think, to plan, to work out complex problems, to be creative, to socialise, to organise. Some of us will be better than others for a variety of reasons. However, we can all improve with practice if we believe in ourself.

Unfortunately, the picture becomes more confusing because a lot of people and organisations use the term talent with a clear indication that talents are innate and they have been defined as **'a special natural aptitude or ability'**. But are they?

Are we once again the victim of our forebears and our hereditary, or do we have some control and influence over our genes?

Listen to the language that we use to support the innate view: 'He is very talented, a natural'. 'She's very gifted'. Those statements immediately suggest that we can never be as good as that person. Whether we can or not does not matter. It is our mindset that is important. We can only control ourself. If we do not put the effort in we will definitely not be able to develop strengths.

For the purpose of this book I use the term strengths as applying to both strengths and talents to reduce confusion, not only yours but also mine. I will leave the debate as to the difference to those engaged in scientific research.

So that we all know what I am talking about, here is a short list of words used by a variety of organisations which are recognised as personal strengths:

Focus	Courageous	Integrity	Authentic	Analytical
Reliable	Humour	Calm	Driven	Flexible
Imaginative	Learner	Enthusiastic	Energetic	Open-minded
Planner	Inspiring	Communicator	Critical thinker	Fairness
Strategic	Persistent	Collaborator	Confident	Resilient

The number of strength words available would fill a book on their own. For practical purposes organisations such as Gallup use 34 strength words, Virtues in Action (VIA) have 24 as do Strengthscope. These are listed in Appendix B. There are many other providers in the market and hundreds of strength words.

Today, when utilising the Mind Fitness process, we work with the four global strengths: awareness, control, focus and feedback in everything we do. The domain strengths identified in our four selves linked to thinking, feeling, driving and social provide a description of how a person will operate in those selves if Mind Fit. These will be discussed in detail in the next chapter. I have found that the more specific strengths buried in each self are more meaningful and effective when people identify their own, and those that they need to develop.

The following diagram demonstrates the direct link between a specific strength through to performance and productivity. Once again, I emphasise that the specific strengths shown at the bottom of the diagram are examples, and individuals, teams and organisations can select different ones to meet specific personal or organisational needs. What is ultimately more important than the strength word, is the description of what it means and the tools and techniques that turn the word into action. For example, strengths such as engaged, structured or driven are important but what brings them to life is knowing 'how to' be engaging, structured or driven.

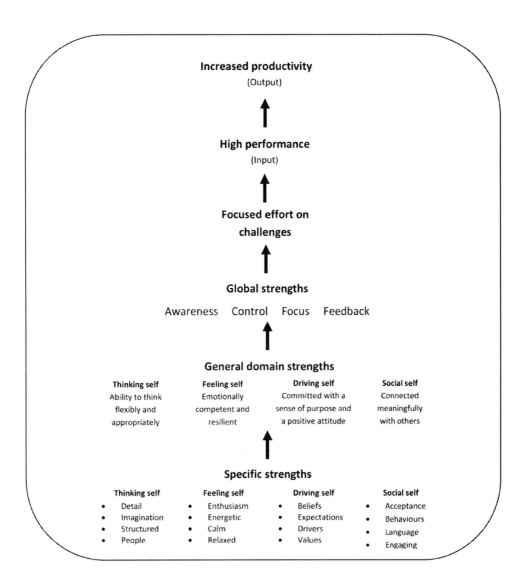

Strengths into action

Here is an example of strength descriptions. To start with I will use the descriptions provided by other organisations. Using courage as an example:

- VIA describes courage as the emotional strengths that involves the exercise of the will to accomplish goals in the face of opposition, both internally and externally. It is composed of bravery, persistence, integrity and vitality.

- Strengthscope defines courage as taking on challenges and facing risks by standing up for what you believe in.

Both descriptions are equally valid but could be meaningless to certain people in specific roles. What do they mean for you and what you do? What if your job is that of a soldier or a fire officer? How would you describe courage? I suspect that the courage these specific roles require is a general courage, whereas, someone who is about to make their first presentation to a board of directors, would need a specific courage for that event.

What about the courage required by a person who is employed, for example, in the world of politics and is aware that certain people are behaving unethically. They need a different form of courage to 'whistle blow' based on their ethics.

The point I am making is that the strength word might be appropriate for different people in different roles but the key to success is to describe that word in the way that makes it meaningful to the individual, team and the organisation. This gives it gravitas.

Let us explore another strength, that of innovation. What does it mean to you? Here are a few descriptions of innovation from the web:

- "A new idea, method or device" (Webster online)

- "Change that creates a new dimension of performance" (Peter Drucker)

- "The introduction of new goods (. . .), new methods of production (. . .), the opening of new markets (. . .), the conquest of new sources of supply (. . .) and the carrying out of a new organization of any industry" (Joseph Schumpeter)

- "Innovation is a new element introduced in the network which changes, even if momentarily, the costs of transactions between at least two actors, elements or nodes, in the network" (Regis Cabral)

- "The ability to deliver new value to a customer" (Jose Campos)

- "Innovation is the way of transforming the resources of an enterprise through the creativity of people into new resources and wealth" (Paul Schumann)

For me, innovation is a new idea, a light bulb moment, a linking of understanding, a paradigm shift. It enables me to make sense of something. That works for me and what I do.

The next stage is to turn an appropriate strength word into practical tools to bring it to life in a way that I like using. Personally, my tools to become innovative are mind maps, future focus, day dreaming, I ask myself questions or simply, I brainstorm. There are many other methods out there. I use whatever appeals to me at the time but there is one important point to make. I practised each of them so that I know exactly what I am doing and not just know about the options. In addition, I know what I am seeking, albeit sometimes without any clarity. I remove distractions which are in my control before I start. I lose myself in the process as I focus on what I am doing.

We are all capable of being innovative. We just have to believe it and practice. What do you believe?

Jessica

Once the belief is changed then the route is clear. This story demonstrates the power of beliefs and the growth of strengths. I was running a workshop for people who had been out of work for a long time. Jessica took part. She was from a run down city estate consisting of poorly maintained social housing. It was made up of large blocks of flats with walkways between and dead ground underneath. Lighting at night was poor and there were always gangs of young people roaming the place. Unemployment and crime was high.

Jessica had not worked for twenty years. She knew that to help her family she had to find work, any work, never mind how menial it was. The company who had organised the workshop insisted that anyone registering on their system for jobs should attend my 'Get Fit for Work' workshop so she had to attend to stand a chance of getting help.

She would not speak out, neither was she able to take part in any of the activities. She sat in a corner with her head down. During a break I had a quiet word with her. Jessica said she did not have any personal strengths and therefore no one would employ her. She had only looked after a home and her family but that was all. She felt worthless. I asked her a series of questions and was amazed to discover that she had brought up nine children. She was extremely proud that none of them had got into trouble with the police. She told me that life had been a struggle especially when her husband was out of work for different periods. Money was very tight, and at times, insufficient.

We explored the strengths needed to run a home, to bring up nine children and make sure that they went to school or whatever activities they were involved in. Finance, time management, personal discipline, relationship builder and collaborator are some of the strengths identified. Adaptable, developer, planner, kindness, organised and emotional control are others. The list went on.

Jessica started to open her eyes as to the strengths she already possessed and had developed over the years without knowing it. I thought what she had achieved in her life was amazing. Then she told me something which was heart stopping and really made me feel humble in her presence. Jessica and a friend would walk the estate at night and confront the gangs of young people. These gangs were drug orientated, violent and carried knives and other paraphernalia used to inflict grievous injuries and worse.

She told me how they would talk to the gang members, never criticised but listened and asked questions. As trust was built they were able to get some gang members to think of the consequences of their actions. Over time, they would ask the gang members to hand over their knives, which many did. That is not only brave beyond belief, but demonstrates a huge number of interpersonal strengths that both ladies possessed.

At the end of the two day workshop Jessica said that her life had been changed. She realised that she had developed many strengths throughout her life which could be use in different jobs and she could learn new ones. Shortly after the workshop she embarked on an administrator's course so that she could work in an office using the strengths that she had together with new ones she later added.

Is it that simple?

Yes. Evidence is mounting today that although strengths do have some genetic element the impact is smaller than many of us believe. There is however, significant evidence to support the premise that our mindset has a significant part to play. In other words, if you want to develop a new strength you have to practice. If you practice for long enough, not only will you develop strengths but ultimately, you can become an expert. You may recall that research over many years has shown that you require about 10,000 hours deliberately practicing something in order to become an expert.

Depending on what strength you are developing, some may require an early start in life. For example, in music as with Mozart, or Formula 1 motor racing as with Lewis Hamilton, early starts were essential. Others can be learnt later in life, such as leadership, personal effectiveness, research techniques and analytical skills.

For most of us, we do not need to become an expert. We just need to become good at something so the amount of effort required is significantly less. How long did it take you to become effective at texting with your thumb? Some of you may say you are not but how much time have you spent practicing or did you give up quickly? If you gave up, what excuse did you make? You have the same innate abilities as someone who can text with their thumb. The difference is what you believe about it and how much focused effort you are willing to put in.

Think about some of the new strengths that you have developed or enhanced over time, for instance, every time you start a new job or are put into a new role. The more often you use a strength, the better you get.

Weaknesses

There is a negative side to what you focus on and practice. For example, if you practice something such as moaning or how to become cynical, you can also get very good at those. No-one is born a moaner or a cynic. It just takes focused practice over a period of time. Conversely, you can keep telling yourself you are no good at something, such as coming up with new ideas or using IT. The result will be as you predicted and as Henry Ford once stated, 'If you believe you can or you believe you can't, you are right'.

I describe weaknesses as '**disempowering beliefs about the possession of innate psychological liabilities, and/or the use of dysfunctional, learned, personal strategies**'. Simply by focusing on and practicing something that has a negative effect we can also become good at them.

In the box below are a small number of weaknesses relating to attitudes and behaviours that impact on us in a negative way.

Avoidance	Can't do	Excuses	Rude	Dominant
Don't know how	Hopelessness	Aggressive	Prevaricator	Moaner
Not bothered	Socially inept	No good	Over controlling	Won't do
Whinging	Shy	Victim	Blame focused	Not my job
Apathy	Powerless	Perfectionist	Cynic	Bully

How many people have you met in organisations like these? How many other negative descriptive words can you identify?

Some people abuse their positional power, or always look for what is not working to their liking, rather than praising for effort. Some may consistently seek to blame others. They learn bullying techniques, become experts at procrastinating or insist on being a perfectionist when perfection is not needed. Others learn to avoid getting involved, to remain separate from others by keeping their heads down or telling everyone they are shy. No-one is born shy. All of these weaknesses have damaging impact on individuals, their colleagues and businesses.

They can all be stopped and changed if a person chooses too.

Salman

Salman was responsible for thirty people and had three team leaders to support him. Over time and unconsciously, he had formed the opinion that everyone in his team was useless resulting in him making all the decisions. He said they even came to him to ask permission to go to the toilet. He spent his whole day making decisions for other people so he had to take his own work home.

It was starting to affect his health and he wanted to know how he could manage himself better. I asked one question which change the way he operated. 'What happens to the business when you go on holiday?' He stared at me for several seconds, then said, 'I am the problem. They just get on with it when I am not there'. Salmon learnt to involve his team members, trust his team leaders and let them make the decisions which are theirs to make. He taught them how to solve problems, analyse data and interpret financial management information. He engaged his staff and they responded positively.

Going back to the beginning

Immediately after the Second World War, Bernard Haldane worked with thousands of veterans from the conflict. He was looking at motivation skills and identified those things that people did well and which gave them energy and joy. Haldane later described these activities as strengths which in his terms were self precepts. In other words, a self belief that you could do something well and were proud of what you did. If you also like doing something it will give you energy and you will get better at it.

Haldane's initial work somehow got lost in time, but, today, other eminent researchers that include Howe, Harrison and Slobada, and more recently K Anders Ericsson, have spent years looking at the innate, or nurtured, side of strengths. The overwhelming evidence is that, although there are small genetic components, strengths are learnt naturally and require focused practice. We are more in control than we think.

In other words, what you practice is what you get. But there is more to what Haldane said. Strengths give you energy and joy. That energy is positive. Today we may use terms such as enthusiastic, excited and happy instead of joy.

Strengths are developed by using our innate assets. We have to believe it and then do it.

Stop playing to your strengths

My second challenge relates to stopping playing only to your strengths and learning to develop new ones which give you that energy and drive, and positive feelings.

Lieutenant David Boyce

This book is dedicated to Lieutenant David Boyce who tragically lost his life in Afghanistan in November 2011. He was only 25 years old. I only knew David for a short time but it was both a delight and a privilege. David served with my son in their regiment, 1st The Queen's Dragoon Guards. They became close friends. I learnt a lot about David and have spoken to his friends, colleagues and family. David is an exemplary example of why we should not only play to our strengths but do different things and seek new challenges, which develop new strengths. Part of David's attitude was that life is an adventure and that you should live it to the full. He continually developed new strengths as a result of the activities he became engaged in. This could be in the sporting arena, education or the army. He quickly became involved in new things and put the effort in to succeed.

David had a 'can do' mindset, was energetic and enthusiastic. He was willing to put the effort in.

The Royal Military Academy at Sandhurst in England challenges young men and women like David to push themselves beyond what they believe they can achieve both physically and mentally. During the punishing year at the academy young people become exceptionally fit, and learn to work in close collaboration with colleagues, whilst at the same time they expand their mental capacity and capabilities. In other words, they develop new strengths.

Whilst exhausted, tired and in the middle of the night they can be tasked with preparing a plan of battle to be executed in two hours. The plan would require using a mass of personal strengths that may result in the ability to handle a lot of information and data, have a vision, assess resource availability and identify the communication methods to be used. And finally, be able to brief the troops accordingly.

Organisations could certainly learn from these young people.

How much wasted time, effort and money take place in organisations today because people do what they have always done? They do not seek to improve themselves or what they are capable of achieving for the organisation

Facing challenges such as those presented at Sandhurst demonstrates that strengths can be developed and placed in usable clusters. If you take the example of preparing a plan in the middle of the night, people need to be resilient, confident, analytical, collaborative, adaptable, decisive, detail oriented, emotionally competent and, of course, courageous. There are also many more strengths that they will use.

The message that I want to give here from David and his colleagues experience of Sandhurst and beyond, are that clusters of strengths can be continually grown and enjoyed if you have a purpose for doing the activity.

David loved being a soldier and wanted to serve his country. As a colleague of David's said, 'Stand down 'Boycey', your duty is done'. He will be sorely missed.

Purpose

We do not have to join the services to develop strengths. What we need is a sense of purpose in what we are doing. Having a purpose generates the drive, commitment and enthusiasm to succeed. It provides the energy to excel. On the journey, by focusing on what is important at that moment in time, you will learn and grow new strengths. This in turn builds real confidence.

The hairdressers

Take a team of ladies hairdressers. When I started working with them they told me that their job was to cut hair. Some might say cutting hair is not very inspiring in itself. As I worked with them, they realised that their job was not only to cut hair, but that by cutting hair well, it gave their clients a sense of well being, pride, worth and pleasure. That is a real sense of purpose.

Take a moment to reflect on what you give to the people you work with and your customers? What is your purpose?

Organisations today need to move away from some of the traditional ways of working. They need to involve, engage and empower people more. Not just talk about it. We need to move away from playing to strengths and give people the opportunity to grow new ones. If they are involved and supported, then they will build their enthusiasm towards the challenge.

Changing negative and self-limiting beliefs and starting to build clusters of strengths in pursuit of challenges moves us away from doing what we have always done. It builds Mind Fitness. What we need to explore now is the four selves that make up Mind Fitness because that enables us to target where to develop strengths and where to put the focused effort in.

CHAPTER 8

Our Four Selves

Quote: 'I cannot teach anyone anything. I can only make them to think.' Socrates 470BC to 399BC

Both the chapter on Mind Fitness and the references to Mind Fitness repeated elsewhere in this book introduced you to the idea that Mind Fitness is made up of our four selves and by optimising our innate assets and potential. The selves relate to how we think, feel, our driving self and our social self. Where do these four selves come from? Put simply, our whole brain. I acknowledge that this description of our brain into four parts has hugely over simplified the complexity of the brain. However, to improve our state of Mind Fitness it requires using a whole brain approach and not just our educational part of it.

To use the whole brain effectively, we need to use our innate assets to think in a flexible and appropriate way. Most people don't think that well. They function and the thinking is often reactive. They will obviously be thinking but it takes place without focus, is constantly shifting and can be based on beliefs, insecurity or dreaming. A lot of people are not driven by their thinking brain but by their emotional and sub conscious brain which often prevents them taking action.

If you don't believe me reflect on what you actually do.

- How much time do you spend thinking in a focused and deliberate way?

- Try listening, carefully, to the conversations of others. Are they based on thinking or beliefs and limited knowledge?

- How often does your thinking take you into the realms of worst case scenario?

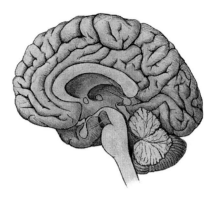

Why are we like this?

We evolved over millions of years. Our emotional brain was one of the first additions to our basic brain structure and helped protect us from external threats. Later we developed parts of the brain related more to learning naturally to survive in a hostile environment and through social support and interactions. A sometimes over simplification of this part of the mind is that of our early Stone Age brain. Very recently we have developed our cognitive capacity to handle and understand data and information, as well as an imaginative ability.

Some people in the field of cognitive psychology still consider that our cognitive ability is the most powerful attribute we have as our actions are based on our mental processing capacity. It potentially could be, but only if used to its full capability. Until quite recently, some scientists argued that beliefs, desires and other mental processes were not real things. This was the view expressed by the behaviourist who stated that cognitive thinking controlled us.

In the 1960s this view began to change. It is obvious to most of us that human beings are complex and our emotions, beliefs, desires, imagination and logical thought all play a significant part in how we operate in our daily lives, both as individuals and in a social setting.

During the 20th century the perceived wisdom was that the brain became a fairly fixed structure after childhood and adolescence. Contrary to this popular belief, the brain actually remains in a state of plasticity throughout our lives. Cellular changes can occur, new neurones develop and new soft wiring put into place. This can be seen following an injury where brain damage occurs. Large scale changes to the brain do result. Brain growth also occurs when playing sport or learning, whether naturally through experiences, or educationally. It grows though practice.

Neuroscience, through brain imaging, is informing us not only how the brain operates but how it operates in areas such as finance, law, decision making and marketing.

Every one of us is genetically and biologically similar, and, for most, our brains hardwired in the same way. What makes each of us different is how we have adapted to the experiences and inputs that we have received and been given throughout our lives. Those experiences for some manifest themselves at the extremes into helpless, defensive or powerful attitudes and behaviours. For most, we will move between all three states depending on the situation.

It is not the intention of this book to go into the realms of science. I leave that to the professionals in their varied fields. I simply want to inform you that although our understanding of how our brains work is increasing it still has a long way to go. However, these new insights are changing the view of how to develop our self. By accepting that knowledge alone does not dictate what we do or how we do it, is a good starting point. Today we require a more global approach to people development: a whole brain approach.

To keep it simple, I have divided the brain into what I describe as our four selves. This enables us to change and develop one small part in one of the selves, en-route to becoming Mind Fit. A change in one part will have an effect across all of the selves as they are linked in a myriad of ways. If you learn through actions to challenge self limiting beliefs then your feelings are likely to become more positive. Your thinking will start to improve and when you speak to people you are likely to be more positive. We just have to make sure that what we change has a positive impact.

Here is my simplistic model of the component parts of the whole brain that we can work with and develop:

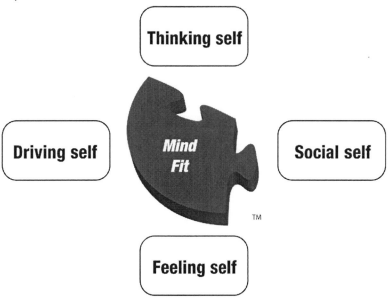

By simplifying the brain in this way it enables us to discover what each part consists of for day to day living and its impact at work, and the necessary area to focus on.

Now is the time to look at the four selves in detail.

Thinking self—the ability to think flexibly and focus appropriately

Our ability to think flexibly and focus appropriately is less developed or used than most of us would like to believe. Neuroscience suggests that when we make instant decisions we are making them from our unconscious and not the modern thinking mind. In other words, from the part of our brain developed and used by early Stone Age people. Some research suggests that 95% of our decisions are made without thinking, and are formed in the unconscious part of the brain from our past experiences, beliefs and attitudes. We instantly produce an answer, right or wrong, without thinking, and are likely to stick to it.

The unconscious mind is also much faster than the more cognitive part of the brain so it can dominate unless we take control. You may recall a quote, 'You can take people out of the Stone Age but you cannot take the Stone Age out of people'.

How often do we come up with answers to a problem without thinking? And once we have made that decision, how easy is it for us to be persuaded to change it? For most of us we stick rigidly to that decision which is a very defensive approach. Yet all it takes, which is a Mind Fit approach, is to acknowledge that instant decision and where it came from and then think. Look for other options, explore the reality and maybe discuss it with others.

Thinking effectively takes conscious thought. Thinking can mean many things such as pondering, reflecting or problem solving. We can think creatively. At its zenith, it is associated with the thinking discipline of philosophy. It is also related to the internal chatter we have within ourself, and the 'critical person' that seems to live inside our heads.

Thinking has a solid feel to it. This is not surprising, since we rely so much on it to make sense of the world we live in. We consider it to be related to a person's level of intelligence. At work we rely on our thinking abilities to create meeting agendas, to conduct appraisals, to make strategic plans, to solve problems and deal with operational issues.

However, the reality is that our thinking is not as controlled as we suppose. People's thinking is often quite rigid, sometimes obsessional. It can be difficult to think in the same way as someone else, making communication difficult. Being aware of, and controlling self-talk and its effects is something few people even consider.

We all develop thinking habits or preferences. The ability to think flexibly is crucial when faced with issues, challenges and working together. Taking control of these thinking habits is a crucial element in Mind Fit development.

A lot of grounded research today has identified four main types of thinking habits: detailed, imaginative, structured and thinking about people. When used singularly they can improve our awareness and become individual strengths. When used together in clusters, across the four types of thinking we really do become effective.

I have put the four main types of thinking into four quadrants. I have also included a small selection of other strengths which complement the four core strengths. There are others.

Detailed	**Imaginative**
Critical	Creative
Decisive	Innovative
Realistic	Open minded
Analytical	Unpredictable
Logical	Non-conforming
Structured	**People**
Predictable	Emotionally involved
Reliable	Communicator
Organised	Empathetic
Controlled	Interpersonal
Methodical	Humanistic

Some people develop or get stuck in one area of thinking because of their job. Others because they enjoy thinking in one particular way. An accountant or an engineer might use detailed strengths found in the top left of the quadrant, whilst a nurse or care worker will probably use thinking strengths from the bottom right. Someone in marketing might operate mainly in the top right imaginative quadrant, whilst an administrator would need structured strengths found in the bottom left.

Learning to use all of these four distinct areas of thinking habits is how we develop the thinking part of Mind Fitness. Which part we use at any moment in time will depend on the situation. Think of a problem, challenge or project that you have at work or at home. To make sure that you have thought through the issue in a flexible and effective way, you need to spend time in each of the quadrants. There is no particular order.

Over the years my preference has moved from imagination to detail as a point to start. This is where a reality check is carried out. What is going on? What information is there? Who is involved? Where can I get more data? Over the years I have found that spending more time in this quadrant pays dividends. It can make all the difference. People are often too eager to come up with solutions even though they have not got all the available facts, sometimes resulting in poor decision taking.

Making sense of the information by structuring it into an understandable form enables it to be built into a plan. It could be put directly into a project management system, a list or into a mind map. Use what works for you or practice something new.

Having a future vision involves your imagination. Thinking outside of the box. Turn ideas on their head. Imagine the future and identify how you got there. Share this imaginary process with others because involving them builds commitment.

The people quadrant is where thinking takes place around other people. It might include thinking about how to involve people. How to communicate the information in a format that others can understand and action. It also includes making sure that the team needs are considered. Failing to think about other people and how to communicate effectively with them, often leads to resistance and ultimately poor performance and failure.

Feeling self—emotionally competent and resilient

Pressure and stress can adversely affect performance, creativity, motivation and communication. It can lead to muddled thinking, irrational decisions and absenteeism. This is costly to organisations in terms of performance and productivity, and costly to the individual in terms of health and quality of life. Conversely, being in control of feelings leads to personal confidence and generates amazing energy, which leads for example, to creativity, better decisions and relationship building.

Can we manage our feelings? The short answer is 'Yes'.

Although popularly referred to as emotional 'intelligence', managing them is actually a learnt ability which results in identifying, experiencing, understanding and expressing human feelings in healthy and productive ways. I use the term 'feelings' as opposed to 'emotions' simply because that is what a person is aware of and experiences at any moment in time. Whilst emotions are always with us, we may not be aware of them.

- How aware are you of your feelings?

- How often are you in a state of negative feelings?

- Do you know what causes those feelings?

- What do you talk about inside your head to keep yourself in that state?

Having a map of our core feelings is a good starting point. In the map below I have identified some of the core feelings that people have regularly expressed. There are many others. Some feelings relate to an immediate threat or positive situation whilst others are caused by past experiences that a person still holds onto. Some relate to moods that we can create and maintain for long periods of time. These are just a small example.

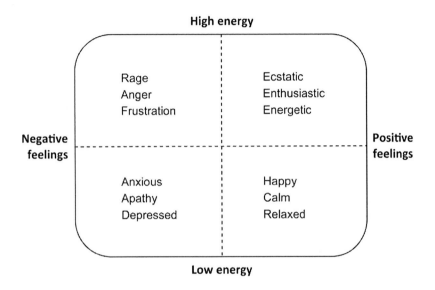

I have just put three feelings in each quadrant as examples. You might like to add your own.

The vertical dimension is the adrenalin input. Sometimes you have low levels whilst at others, you might be buzzing. The horizontal dimension relates to hormones which give you completely opposite feelings. The negative hormones are often linked with fear and anxiety whilst the positive ones create a sense of well being. The latter are often associated with being in 'flow' or in the 'zone'.

Being emotionally competent requires the learnt ability to move from a negative state to a positive one. The tools and techniques to achieve this have a major impact on our commitment and the flexibility of our thinking, as well as our ability to operate socially in a positive way.

Controlling our feelings is easier that many people think. I have had great success with this from the unemployed through to chief executives, from shy people to those who have been unable to control their anger.

First, become aware of your feelings. Next is to understand what triggers those feelings and surprisingly, although some are external, many stem from inside of us. They are formed from our beliefs about a situation and our ability to deal with it. Once the cause and its origins have been identified, then it is simply a matter of using one of the many tools and techniques that we each have, often without knowing it. The tools to manage feelings generally fall into three types. I have given some examples in each of the types. There are a myriad of others.

1. Physical

    a. Standing tall and smiling

    b. Taking a walk

    c. Breathing slowly

2. Imaginary

    a. Take yourself to a good place, for example a holiday location

    b. Create the perfect state of feeling good in your mind

    c. Lower your centre of gravity in your mind and note how grounded you become

3. Social

    a. Talk to a friend

    b. Seek professional support

    c. Have a rule of no moaning to others

We all know of these or other similar tools and techniques. Unfortunately, most of us do not practice them. What people do tend to practice are imaginary disaster scenarios and they keep replaying them over and over in their mind. Some people beat themselves up inside their heads by self talk that is destructive, others by only communicating with negative like minded people in a way which maintains apathy or frustration.

Once you have identified what works for you in a positive way, focus on it and practice. Try mixing a physical and an imaginary tool together. It can transform your life.

Driving self—committed with a sense of purpose and a positive attitude

Buried in our sub consciousness are the key factors which provide us with meaning for what we do. Without them life can be a real struggle and not very enjoyable. Becoming Mind Fit requires some time thinking about those aspects of your life that give you the energy you need to enjoy life to the full. It might sound complicated. However, with a little bit of thought, you will be amazed at what you can discover.

1. Beliefs and expectations

In our driving self we find our beliefs and expectations, drivers and values. All of these impact on what we do, and how we do it, without realising it. I have dedicated a chapter to beliefs because they are so important and so powerful. As you go through this book you might start to recognise the power of your own beliefs and how they can control you in both a positive and a negative way.

Expectations are simply beliefs about what to expect in the future. Personal expectations need to be realistic. Unrealistic expectations can have a negative impact on what people do as they may strive to achieve something which is not attainable.

Mind Fit people spend time identifying their beliefs and expectations simply by thinking about them. Try this when faced with a problem or a situation you have not come across before: simply ask yourself a few questions:

- What do I believe about this (situation/person)?

- Where is the evidence to support my beliefs?

- What evidence is there to show me I am wrong?

It can be an amazing experience as it opens our eyes. We discover new things about people and situations. We start to challenge what we hear or read. It enriches us. We think.

A report that hit the media recently said that some people have a genetic variation which results in them 'needing' more sleep. It was not long before I heard a lot of people saying that they have that gene which is why they stay in bed until mid to late morning. People responded to the headline in the way that they wanted to hear it because it suited them. It turned out to be only partially true as there are many other factors to be taken into consideration.

A professor who responded to the report said that there is a tiny genetic variation but it has nothing to do with needing sleep or needing to stay in bed for hours. Sleep is affected by many variables that include what we eat and drink, what is going on in our life, the quality of our bed, our physical state and most importantly, the quality of our sleep. Deep sleep is essential to feeling refreshed in the morning. Unless we have that deep sleep we may want to stay in bed longer. It does not always work. Controlling our life and the quality of our sleep is more important than the tiny genetic variation which has a minimal effect.

Some people only heard what they wanted to believe.

2. Personal drivers

Understanding what motivates or drives people to certain courses of action remains a bit of a mystery. We know that some people have a strong need for security whilst others seek adventure and take enormous risk. Whatever those drivers are, they are buried deep inside our mind and are personal to each one of us. They help shape our lives. This is why each of us can benefit by thinking about and understanding our significant personal drivers and how they impact on our lives. Drivers provide our motivation, commitment and sense of purpose.

One group of personal drivers has been identified from research include: freedom, security, learning, leisure, creation, identity, curiosity and participation. There are others. To satisfy a personal driver you might join a sports team or a social club. You might choose to work in a particular form of employment or volunteer for a chosen cause. Curiosity could take you into history or philosophy, and identity might lead you to researching your family's past. Pursuing a personal driver gives people a real sense of purpose and satisfaction.

How many drivers have you got? How can or does work satisfy some of these drivers either directly or indirectly?

The more conscious links we can make between those deeply held drivers to all aspects of our lives provides a real sense of purpose. Mind Fit people seek these drivers because they know that doing something which has meaning provides positive energy, persistence and determination.

3. Values

At one level we can name those values which are important to us personally and collectively. However, when it comes to describing what each one actually means to other people it becomes rather difficult, let alone how we live by them. It seems like trying to grip a bar of wet soap. Honesty to me can mean something totally different to you. The same applies to friendship or loyalty and so on.

There are many value words that include:

- Friendship

- Loyalty

- Trust

- Democracy

- Respect

- Ethical practices

- Honesty

- Relationships

- Pleasure

- Openness

In the past I have participating in training programmes where so much time has been spent examining values to identify the meaning which has ultimately been a waste of time. Simply because values and what they mean to us is buried deep inside each of us, they are very personal. Only when we believe that a value is not being met will we notice it.

To overcome this complexity, identify a set of describable behaviours through the creation of a set of ground rules that we can live by at work and elsewhere. Think about your own values and the behaviours that come from them. What behavioural ground rules would you live by? Here are a couple to start you off:

- I do what I say I will do

- I always support my work colleagues

Simple rules like these, when agreed by a work team, can completely change the culture at work. By living and working by the agreed rules, many of the difficult to describe values will be catered for.

The social self—connecting meaningfully with others

The social self, or as it is sometimes called social intelligence, is the collective output of the three previous selves: thinking, feeling, and our drivers. The social self is the ability to get along with others and, where relevant, to co-operate and collaborate together—willingly.

Many people are blind to their social self. Those who have learned to be helpless may avoid social events or if defensive, may assess themselves, wrongly, as being highly competent in the social environment. People often have a low awareness of their own abilities and the impact their communication style can have on others. They often associate with like-minded people, therefore reinforcing their mindset. Some people, who may have a toxic style of interaction, leave others feeling devalued, angry, frustrated, or helpless in a given situation. Others sometimes leave people feeling drained or confused.

To be competent in our social self we need to ensure that we operate effectively across all component parts that make up Mind Fitness, and not just some. Mind Fit people vary their approach according to others needs as well as their own. Their high level of awareness enables them to assess people and situations, linked with a range of interaction styles. In this way they are able to connect appropriately.

Mind Fit people spend time with other people. They can simply listen or inspire and engage. They accept people for what they are. They use language that is appropriate and ensures that what is being discussed is understood. This does not mean that they go out of their way to like people who are socially inept but they will treat them in the same way as any other person. Remember, the purpose of being socially fit is to connect meaningfully with others.

Understanding our social self is crucial. 'Connecting' includes the ability to understand other people: how they think, what they are feeling, what drives them, and how to work co-operatively with them.

People, who operate well in the social self, are highly aware of themselves and others, and behave and use language appropriately in different contexts. At work, this can be with a colleague, as a team member or leader. It can make a big impact on sales and customer service.

The surge in social networking is a clear indication that we need to be competent in our social self. Whether at a local breakfast meeting or using a web based tool, we need to engage this new phenomenon. We are communicating more than ever before.

Yet the basics have not changed. We need to be open minded, to listen, to ask questions. We need to show an interest in the other person, who they are and what they do and what they aspire to? Communicating effectively is simply ensuring that a significant part of the focus is on the other person and not only our self. In a work context this is still achievable. Focusing on people's needs as well as those of the organisation and team is what communicating is about. Without it, connecting meaningfully will remain a struggle.

The following diagram summaries the four selves that make up Mind Fitness together with the descriptive component strengths that effective use of specific strengths can achieve.

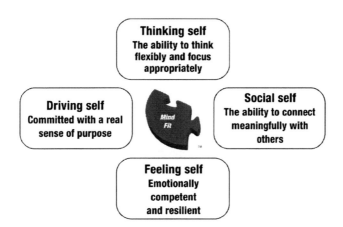

Each part of our four selves is interlinked which, as you may recall from Chapter 6 on complex adaptive systems, is why a small positive or negative change in one part will impact throughout the whole. Beware that drivers will become blockers in a negative state.

Which strengths?

At the beginning of the book I made reference to list of strengths provided by organizations that help you identify your strengths through questionnaires. The ones I identified are Gallup which has a list of 34, VIA 24 and Strengthscope also 24. A total of 82 strengths (see Appendix B for the full list). There are other providers and a good book on strengths is 'A Psychology of Human Strengths', details of which are provided in Appendix C.

What is interesting is that you can take every one of these individual strengths and drop them into one of the four selves. Here are some examples, one from each provider:

- Gallup—**Empathy** (Social self). Can sense the feelings of other people by imagining themselves in others' situations.

- Strengthscope—**Efficiency** (Thinking self). Taking a well-ordered and methodical approach to tasks to achieve planned outcomes.

- VIA—**Learner** (Driving self). Have a great desire to learn and want to continuously improve.

These examples clearly demonstrate the practical application of the four selves as a way of understanding how we operate. It provides a more elegant approach than that of a list of strength words. By placing an identified strength in a structure gives each of us more understanding, choice and control which can be linked to personal and business improvement.

Of course the best strengths are the ones which we have identified ourself and which contain a description that is meaningful to us.

Using strengths from external providers may be a useful starting point from which to explore personal strengths, but there is a danger to it. One company I worked with had used a personal profiling tool to ensure they employed people for a particular role with a virtually identical profile. The organization was subsequently amazed that this particular group with similar characteristics all performed differently. Some better than others. When I spoke to the group members it caused me to ask them a question, 'Are the identified strengths really you or have you changed to fit the profile?' This left them pondering.

Identifying and developing our own strengths is ultimately far more meaningful and powerful. I would recommend that you start with the driving self because that has very strong links with the other three. I will give you a personal example of two drivers from my deep self and what they mean for me.

- Freedom – to roam, to think, to have choice, to be involved, to say no.

- Curiousity – to explore, to ask, to share, to research, to know.

These personal drivers have led me to improve my capacity to think in a variety of ways, to share and be a better leader. Also to control and understand my emotions as these two drivers are linked for me to positive feelings.

If you choose to identify strengths in each of your four selves I suggest you start with no more than four in each self. Reflect on the strength word. What does it mean for you? What tools do I use to activate it?

Then build your own personal strength profile.

Health warning

A lot of time is spent on identifying personal strengths in different organizations so that people play to their strengths. This can cause or create a situation which is not always healthy for other people or the organization.

A managing director of a company had overly developed thinking strengths based on innovative approaches to building his business and an ability to handle a mass of complex detail. Unfortunately, he had failed to develop two other thinking strengths based on organizing and communicating those ideas and the detail around them. To make sense of his ideas he needed to develop a structure which was meaningful to other people. He failed to do this. The result was a confused and disengaged group of people who did not understand what he was saying or how to deliver what was required. They felt frustrated and inadequate. His overplay on limited strengths became business critical.

Whatever strengths you have or choose to develop, it is important to consider links and consequences. We are all very complex. Ensure that those strengths you have chosen give you an all round capability, as overplay on a small number of strength can be damaging.

It is also worth spending time on those perceived weaknesses that we all have and putting them into the four selves. The reason is simple: you will then know which ones to stop. If you identify moaning as a social weakness then you can simply stop moaning and replace it with something positive.

One final point to reinforce on strengths is that if you believe they are innate, if they were given to you at conception, then what neuroscience is telling us about the brains capability to develop new pathways and neurons is wrong. Neuroplasticity of the brain which informs us that it remains malleable throughout our life is also wrong. That our biology does not respond to the environment but only to our internal demands. Such beliefs will stop you dead in the water.

If those beliefs were true then what would be the point of education, of learning, of developing? Would it not be simpler to develop a system which identifies innate talents and then program people to spend their lives doing what those innate talents enable?

We are all much more than our genes.

Without doubt, I am on the side of nurture in the debate. I do acknowledge that it is not all nurture and that nature has a significant part to play. My findings from the research that I do, are that the pendulum is significantly swinging towards nurture and that until we tap into our real potential we will never discover our limit. Neither do I accept that it is nurture OR nature. I take the view that it is our genes multiplied by the environment.

When something happens in our environment, for example, someone makes a sexist or racist remark, or you hear on the news that a cruise liner has toppled over in the Mediterranean with 4000 people on board, what response takes place inside of you? You have responded to an external event. In addition, we create in our minds our own external environment by imagining all different scenarios. Some good and some bad.

Martin Seligman's Virtues in Action (VIA) lists 24 strengths linked to human virtues. Seligman's research work covers the learned states of helplessness, optimism, happiness and flourish, and therefore, he clearly supports the premise that we can learn both strengths and weaknesses by attributing external events to our life.

Once you have identified your own strengths and removed or reduced weaknesses you will move upwards on the Personal Profile Map®. The following diagram represents the three states of mind UN-Fitness namely Helplessness, Defensiveness and Mind Fitness state leading to Personal Power. Each of the boxes by those states represents strengths and weakness relating to how we think, feel, what drives us or blocks us and our social self. It is what happens between these three states that we need to understand. This is the map that we need to explore next.

'The Personal Profile Map® with its three states.

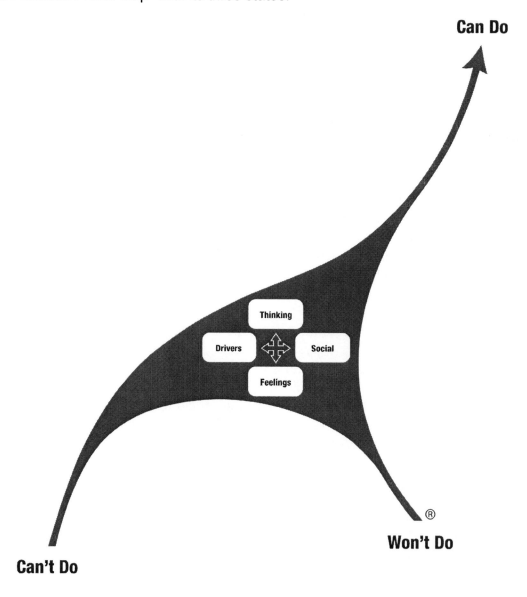

CHAPTER 9

Personal Profile Map®

Quote: 'You must be the change you are seeking in the world.' Mahatma Gandhi

By now it is obvious that high performance, whether personal or tangible, is the result of a person having the ability to operate effectively and efficiently across all the four selves which make up Mind Fit. This is the state that leads to a person having a 'can do' attitude, increased confidence, emotional resilience and the ability to connect meaningfully with people. In this chapter we will explore those key aspects that lead to high performance and provide you with a useful route map, the Personal Profile Map®, for your onward journey to exceptional results.

Personal Profile Map®

The London Underground Map

Imagine you are a tourist in London and have just spent a pleasant morning visiting London Zoo in Regents Park. You decide to spend the afternoon visiting the Tower of London next to the Thames. The medieval structure which contains the famous White Tower was commenced by William the Conqueror shortly after 1070AD. Something you would like to see whilst in London.

The easiest way to get there is to take the underground from Camden Town, the nearest station to the Zoo and leave at Tower Hill Station for the Tower of London. You have to travel south and east. However, here is the twist. Imagine taking the journey without an underground map. Maps of the underground do not exist. All you have is a list containing the names of the 270 stations that make up the tube network which also covers a distance of 249 miles on 14 different lines. I will give you one further piece of information. The start and end station are on different lines.

Confused?

The message I am giving is that without a map you could be travelling around the London Underground for days or you might be lucky and make the change you need at the right station whilst travelling in the right direction first time.

For those of you who have never seen the London Underground map just look it up on the web. You will see a map which informs you of all the information you need to travel around the network effectively. The map however, is a long way from being geographically accurate. It was never intended to be. The original designer of the map in 1931 was Harry Beck, an unemployed electrical draughtsman. He produced a purely representational diagram with no surface detail except the stations and a stylised River Thames.

With its out-of-scale distances the map was originally rejected. However, in 1933 the map was accepted and although it has been continually tinkered with since, the public have accepted it totally. It works. It makes sense. Maps do not have to be accurate to be informative and effective.

The Personal Profile Map®

The Personal Profile Map® is much like the London Underground Map. It is a representation of some of the core and complex science and aspects that makes us human with all our similarities and uniqueness. The research behind it comes from gems that were identified from over 100 scientific papers. I explored different psychologies including evolutionary, clinical, sport and positive psychology. I also broadly looked at biology, neuroscience and neuroplasticity, genetics and epigenetic. In addition, I explored some of the non traditional offerings which are in the market but which have little or obsolete science behind them. They include neuro-linguistic programming (NLP), hypnosis and transactional analysis (TA).

The gems I discovered formed a pattern from which the profile map was constructed.

It has now been shared with people from all walks of life and the one constant I have received from them over the last 14 years, is that it makes sense. It is intuitively right.

Once people understand the map for themselves, it enables people to quickly identify if they are sliding down one of the curves and in what direction, or if they are operating between the two negative states at the bottom of the map.

The peculiar shape of the map is made up of the three core states of being Helpless, Defensive and Powerful. The map is based on three standard deviation curves which have been put together with a large degree of poetic licence. Extreme states are at the end of each curve and in reality most of us will operate in and around the middle of the map. Every one of us will, to some degree, move up, down, around and across the map depending on the current situation and our perception of it. It is when a person gets stuck in one of the negative states that major problems can occur. Unfortunately, too many people today consistently operate in the bottom half of the map.

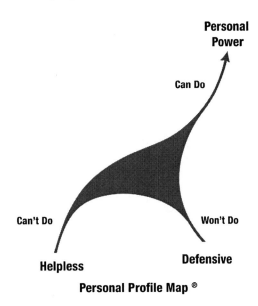

Personal Profile Map ®

It is important to remind you that the three states at each end of continuums and throughout the map are all learnt naturally. They are actually pronounced as Learned Helplessness, Learned Defensiveness® and Learned Powerfulness®. This also applies to the strengths, weaknesses, attitudes and behaviours which can be found at any point on the map and which we will explore next.

Learned Helplessness

This state is an excellent starting point from which to build our understanding of how people operate in broad terms across the map. I intend to make reference to two experiments by Ivan Pavlov, and Martin Seligman and his colleague, Steve Maier. I have however, simplified what are complex experiments for the sake of expediency as this book is not about those experiments but the fallout from them.

First, let us consider Ivan Pavlov's experiments on dogs which took place between 1890 and 1930. He recognised that dogs salivate when food is presented, which is what one would expect. However, by ringing a bell before the dogs received their food, the dogs subsequently learnt to associate the bell with food. The outcome was that after several repetitions they salivated when the bell was rung. He called this classical conditioning. The bell became a stimulus which caused a response. The learning being that there is a cause which has a direct response effecting to the outcome.

Martin Seligman's work took place in the late 1960s and the early 1970s. He experimented on dogs where one group were placed in a harness from which they could not escape and were subjected to a series of electric shocks. These dogs were 'conditioned' to take the shocks and subsequently, laid down and took them. They were helpless as they had no control over their situation.

Later, those same dogs were placed in a box from which they could easily escape by jumping a barrier. Although some did jump, the great majority stayed where they were and took the electric shocks. These dogs, which had learnt to become helpless in one scenario and applied that learning to a different situation. A situation from which they could escape but did not. This experiment demonstrated that the behaviour does not necessarily have to be directly related to the cause. The learning that had taken place could be applied anywhere to any situation.

Later, it was recognised through further experiments on people, this time without electric shocks, that the same outcome resulted. When people feel that they have no control over their situation, they may begin to behave in a helpless manner by not changing when opportunities arrive. This inaction, in extremes cases, can lead to people becoming not only helpless, but depressed.

The state can result for example, in a child who has done badly in a maths or English test to believe that they can do nothing about it. It is outside of their control and when faced with a similar situation the sensation of helplessness overrides everything and they once again perform badly.

People at work who have a manager who makes all the decisions, may feel a sense of helplessness as control of what they do has been removed from them. They may subsequently doubt their own ability to deliver and only do what they are told. They often avoid putting themselves in positions where they have to take any responsibility which in turn reinforces the manager's decision that the person is not up to the job. All because the perceived control has been removed from them, resulting in a less motivated and disengaged workforce.

A state of helplessness often manifests itself in underperformance, passive disengagement, apathy and stress at work.

The condition can also affect social situations. If people have bad experiences in the social arena they may feel inadequate in all such situations and start to believe that they are not good at building and maintaining relationships. One outcome is to accept that they are naturally shy thus making shyness behaviour even more pronounced. A term for shyness which is gaining in popularity is social anxiety. It is a learnt behaviour and can be unlearnt and replaced by something positive: if the person chooses too.

Other research suggests that people who have learnt to become helpless, attribute this to three characteristics which explain their failure. They are:

- The cause of failure is **internalised** by the individual. They believe they are the problem. If something has failed the fault is down to that individual. Their world is one of insecurity. They believed they are no good at most things which may cover IT, presentation skills, social events or they have lost their confidence.

- Failure frequently occurs because the situation is always negative and never really changes. It always goes wrong. For example, a person genuinely believes that every time they buy an electrical appliance, it will not work. They are jinxed.

- Finally, they believe that most situations are uncontrollable. There is nothing they can do about it. Life is like that. A frequently heard saying is that 'life is a bitch and then you die'. If anything goes right for these helpless people they put it down to luck. It cannot be any other reasons because they know that they have no control over a situation.

The Personal Profile Map® below shows some of the characteristics which can be found in this part of the map. These are just a very small selective sample. Many other descriptive words could be used here.

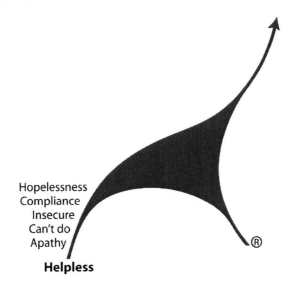

Hopelessness
Compliance
Insecure
Can't do
Apathy

Helpless

The overwhelming state of a person operating from a helpless place is that they are powerless which is caused by a sense of being out of control.

People who operate consistently in the helpless part of the map will be passively disengaged at work. Figures on engagement suggest that up to 60% of people in work today may fall into this state to some degree. The current economic climate will undoubtedly produce more people who slip down towards helplessness. They will have very little energy and what they do have will be negative. The result will be that they take very little action to change their position.

In my terms, these people see the world as a bad place where most things go wrong and most of the time they believe it is their fault. They have lost control of themselves.

The receptionist

Louisa was a receptionist for her local health authority in their main office building. I later learnt that she had worked for the authority for several years and had a terrible sick and poor performance record.

I was sitting in the reception area waiting for a meeting to take place when I heard a colleague of hers ask her how she was. Louisa immediately started to recite how terrible things were. She started with her back which was a bit better than yesterday. She was worried how she would carry the shopping home as she always drops things. Wasn't the weather terrible? The news headlines are always dreadful. It seems to be getting worse. She went on and on.

Louisa's tone of voice was drab and depressive. She had no physical or mental energy. She looked and sounded drained.

I could not help notice her colleagues face which was a picture. It said, 'I wish I had never asked'.

Learned Defensiveness®

People who have learnt to operate in a defensive state have a totally different approach to how they can survive and sometimes thrive in life, albeit in a selfish way. It is an approach based on taking control. In fact the more they can control the better.

They do however share two of the three characteristics found in Learned Helplessness.

- Failure frequently occurs because the situation is always negative and never really changes. It always goes wrong.

- They believe that the situation is uncontrollable. There is nothing they can do about it. Life is like that.

The third characteristic is completely different. It is:

- The cause of failure is **external** as they believe the factors have their origin with others. The fault is down to other people and not the defensive person. How can it be? They know best.

Underneath, a defensive person has a sense of vulnerability. To overcome this negative state they tend to seek to over-control everything they do. This is why such people have a very rigid mindset. A statement they might make is 'I have made up my mind, don't confuse me with the facts'.

They may become jobs worths, never putting themselves out for others. They will constantly criticise, seek fault, prevaricate and blame. As leaders, many may become loud and aggressive or quietly stubborn. They are very difficult to deal with. Bullying can be part of their repertoire, whether at work or at home. Their over controlling attitude and behaviour can cause some people to develop a sense of helplessness.

But they have a weakness, where once it is opened, they can succumb to a loss of control rapidly. When exposed defensive people sometimes collapse as the foundation on which they have built their bravado is weak. Their foundation is their vulnerability. Once defensive people acknowledge that their existing attitude and behaviour has destructive and debilitating consequences, they can and surprisingly most do, become the most positive and productive people.

This map shows some of the many characteristics that defensive people might exhibit.

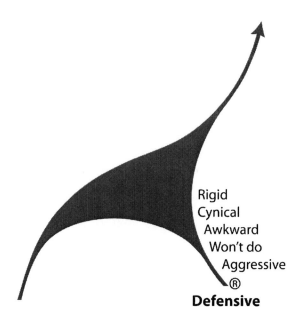

Rigid
Cynical
Awkward
Won't do
Aggressive
®
Defensive

The overwhelming need of a defensive person is to be in control, to dominate and protect their vulnerability. Once again the descriptive words used are a selective few. There are a myriad of other words which could be used.

The store man

Steve, the store man in a manufacturing company, would not let anything out of his store unless the paperwork was completed to his liking. It was at a time convenient to him and where the stock was delivered to, was wherever he fancied leaving it. Most unhelpful. He was also a big man with a loud voice and a vicious tongue which aggravated the situation as people tended to avoid him.

Steve took part in a Mind Fit workshop. He was initially his typical self, loud and brazen. However, as the characteristics of a defensive person were explored, Steve went quiet. Suddenly he put his hands up in surrender and said 'I'm sorry'. He told the group that he had no idea how his attitude and behaviour impacted on people and the business. He said he wanted to change for the better and asked team members to support him. Steve quickly became an integral player in changing the culture of the company and providing what people wanted, when they wanted it and where they needed it.

Mind Fitness leads to Learned Powerfulness®

You may recall that a few of the dogs in the experiments by Martin Seligman did escape from their traumatic situation and avoided being electrocuted. What was different with these dogs that caused them to take positive action? We do not know. However, we can explore and consider how a person who operates with a sense of Personal Power will behave.

Let us start with how they attribute success or failure compared with a helpless and defensive person.

- Success is generally the result of the individual taking action in areas that they can control or have influence over.

- Most things go right and when they don't, failures are usually caused by events outside of the individual's control.

- Because most things that occur are a mix of predictable and unpredictable, then what we do and how we do it can influence the outcome.

People who are Mind Fit and operate from a sense of Personal Power have a real sense of purpose. They not only want to develop themselves but grow other people. They operate from a sense of humility rather than arrogance sometime found within defensive people.

The map shows some of the characteristics of a powerful person but, as with the previous two states, there are many more.

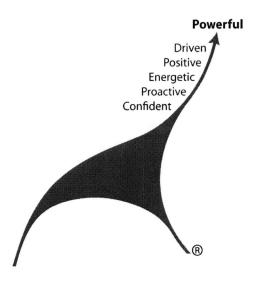

Personal Power is a state of being that we can all achieve with focused effort. The source of this power comes from within. It has a real sense of being grounded. This Personal Power does not come from an external source such as position, having information or expertise in a particular field. Neither does it stem from the ability to reward or punish people or control people. It is simply a state of being that provides a variety of positive strengths that include confidence, drive, resilience and contentment. They have high levels of positive energy; they think and can remain calm. Humility is often found at its core.

People operating from this state have a sense not only of self worth but in turn, they value other people. They are driven to help people develop and take responsibility for their actions.

Mind Fitness is the route to this state.

The speech therapist

Juggling two teenage children, a husband and a home, plus a job that has a lot of responsibility, caused Pauline to feel in a constant state of being overwhelmed. This was mixed with a need to take control of everything she was doing. When things did not go to her plan she would feel frustrated and take it out on those people close to her.

She often felt out of control and had learnt that the only way to manage her life was to over control everyone around her. That included her family, the administrative support at work, her young clients and their parents. She was continually orientating between a helpless and a defensive state.

Nothing ever went right. Her children would not get ready for school fast enough. Traffic to work was always heavy with constant jams and clients would not arrive on time making the situation more pressurised.

Following a workshop on Mind Fitness she realised that she was trying to do things in the same way that she had always done them when life was easier, when she seemed to have more control. Today, her children were growing up, traffic had increased, and the number of clients she was expected to meet had also gone up. She started her day with a mindset that things would go wrong and she would end up stressed.

She had to take control of the one thing she could control: herself. She decided that by getting up 15 minutes earlier she would get everything in place that she needed before the family sat down for breakfast. She provided what they needed and left responsibility of getting to school to her children. She left home a few minutes earlier with a positive mindset, and if she got stuck in heavy traffic then there was nothing she could do about it. If needed, she could phone the office to advise them if she was going to be delayed.

Pauline now arrived at work with a 'can do' mindset. As she got better at controlling her feelings, and her thinking became more positive, she found that her social interactions also improved. Over time, she was able to increase the number of clients she saw everyday by focusing on what was important and not ranting about those things that were outside of her control.

CHAPTER 10

The Core Sources And Science

Quote: 'To try and fail is at least to learn. To fail to try is to suffer the inestimable loss of what might have been.' Chester Bernard

Particularly in the early days, things did not always go as planned. For example, linking natural learning with educated learning proved a nightmare as knowledge always prevailed. But for me that is good feedback. Learning did take place and more and more theories were examined and the gems taken out which gradually built into the constructed map from the previous chapter.

In this chapter I want to share with you some of the sources and theories that sit behind Mind Fitness, which I initially explored with Dr Alan Beggs some of whose work is included here. I have continued the journey which remains on-going. For those who are not interested in the science this chapter is not essential.

Although the process to develop Mind Fitness does not involve theories which are a cognitive approach, some of you may be curious to know where the science comes from. This chapter is a snapshot of the whole, and will point you in the right direction should you wish to know more.

The nature of theories

It is important to acknowledge that theories are not the truth. They are the result of some highly focused thinking by some very intelligent people. It is best to think of them as 'best guesses', based on their insights and the data they have at their disposal at a point in time. As time moves on, new information and research evidence changes the previous findings. Science is a robust and effective process which aims to test these guesses, to either affirm theories or test them to destruction.

In most theories there is a gem of an idea even if the theory itself has been superseded. Many of those gems have been collected and collated from a wide range of theories and linked to practical approaches. Research from different psychologies including occupational, health, evolutionary and sports forms the backbone of Mind Fitness. Biology, neuroscience, neuroplasticity, epigenetic and quantum mechanics have also been explored at a more general level

Mind Fitness approach

Because of this eclectic approach, Mind Fitness on its own is not a revolutionary theory. It is a construct built from the gems of the best theories. Many of the tools and techniques used to become more Mind Fit are also well-known. What is new is the combination of ideas drawn from several diverse fields in a coherent and over-arching model and process, the Personal Profile Map®, the use of the whole brain and the deliberate use of natural learning.

The Personal Profile Map® provides individuals with a route map. The map enables people to plot their current position on it, and through focused effort it will lead to higher levels of Mind Fitness, work performance and well-being.

The Mind Fitness process also enables an individual to develop or improve personal strengths. Ultimately, it leads to hidden knowledge, acquired implicitly through natural learning. You know how to do something but find it difficult to describe.

However, mixing implicit (natural) and explicit (educated) learning at the same time does not work very well. It is for this reason I never share the underpinning theory of the process with workshop participants to avoid the cognitive mind dominating the thought process. This is one of the uniqueness of the Mind Fit process. Where explicit knowledge is required it needs to follow the initial Mind Fit development. In practice these can be concurrent activities but a significant break should be built in. This could simply mean they are separated by a part of a day or better still a whole day.

The business case

Throughout this book I have used sources from various web based sites and professional bodies to outline some of the background to the business case for this new approach. They cover topics such as underperformance, sickness, disengagement and conflict. These sources include the Health & Safety Executive in the UK, the Chartered Institute of Personnel and Development and Gallup. There are many more which are regularly updated. I would however, recommend that you conduct your own checks as the figures stated are constantly changing, albeit there appears to be a general consistency and trend.

Biannual research by Gallup over many years has found a fairly consistent number of people who felt disengaged at work. Although percentages do change they suggest that the number of engaged people at work, the 'can do' people, varies from 20% to 30%, whilst the passively disengaged, the 'can't do' people, shifts between 54% and 59%. The actively disengaged, the 'won't doers', who have a more militant stance, shifts between 17% and 19%. These figures vary between countries.

My own experience and research with people at work found that a similar percentage felt disempowered and had become disengaged as a result. I wanted to obtain some theoretical leverage on this and looked for psychological models which might shed some light on why such a large number of people are disengaged.

Performance theories

In Chapter three I looked at personal performance and gave a specific approach based on what people do at any moment in time and not what they achieve. Much of my thinking on performance stems from sport where psychological factors to performance have been accepted for decades.

David Hemery won a Gold medal at the 1968 Olympic Games in Mexico for the 400 metre hurdles. I have spent a lot of time with David and he was one of the athletes who explained to me about the importance of performance being focused on the input.

Suzanne Kubasa suggested that from sport the three characteristics needed to perform are based on what she describes as hardiness. They are control, commitment and challenge. Later, research from Hull University developed a model based on mental toughness that was related to performance under pressure. They added confidence to Kubasa's model of hardiness. Sian Beilock's (2010) book entitled *Choke* refers to the secret of performing under pressure and provides some new insights from the field of brain development.

K Anders Ericsson and his team (1993) from Florida University explain the role of deliberate practice in the acquisition of expert performance. This activity based practice limits the role of innate characteristics and it clearly links performance. Deliberate practice is the total focus on the activity which can lead to a state described as 'Flow' by Mihaly Csiksentmihalyi (1990). He stated:

> **'In our studies we found that every flow activity, whether it had involved competition, chance or other dimension of experience had this in common: it provided a sense of discovery, a creative feeling of transporting the person to a new reality. It pushes the person into higher levels of performance and led to undreamed states of consciousness. In short, it transformed the self by making it more complex. In this growth of the self lies the key to flow activities.'**

People in flow have a sense of purpose, clear goals, and the knowledge and skills required to perform the task. They immerse themselves in the activity, focus their attention on what they are doing at that moment in time, and receive constant feedback. As a result of the experience, they lose sense of time, and the task becomes effortless and enjoyable.

Williams and Krane (2000) described optimal performance as a state when people feel in total control, totally focused on the task, extremely confident, and with a total loss of self consciousness. Their perception of the passage of time is altered either by losing all awareness of time, or feeling that time has slowed down.

Thinking is clearly associated with performance. The concept of multiple cognitive skills, those personal support strategies which are known to be closely associated with performance in several areas (e.g. Covington, 1985; Richardson, 1978) is also important. Unfortunately, many people fail to plan, set targets, or prioritise.

Nideffer's (1976) work on Attentional Style provided new insights. Many people get locked into a too detailed style, and miss the big picture—or stay locked inside their head, listening to self-talk or drifting off to another time or place. A Mind Fit person will understand this, and be able to shift attention (or focus) as required.

Personal Profile Map®

The original bipolar model used was based on one continuum or standard deviation linking Learned Helplessness and Learned Powerfulness® at the extremes. That continuum was inadequate to describe or explain the controlled negativity of some individuals as it did not include what today I refer to as Learned Defensiveness®.

By combining Rotter's (1966) work on 'Locus of Control', which is a theory in personality psychology referring to the extent to which individuals believe that they can control events from either an internal or external perspective; with Frankel and Snyder's (1978) work on self-protective defensiveness, this became represented by the defensive branch on the Personal Profile Map®. This third extreme state completes the links between Learned Helplessness, Learned Defensiveness® and Learned Powerfulness®

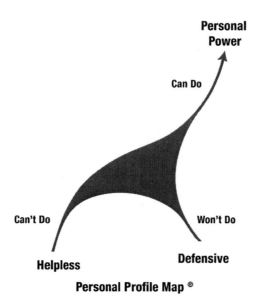

Personal Profile Map ®

This purely graphical representation of the three states is intuitively satisfying to most people. It was never meant to be a testable model, simply a 'road-map' which helps in the exploration of Mind Fitness. It also enables people to self assess and plot their own consistent state or the degree of personal flex within and across the map.

Natural learning

To increase Mind Fitness, a person may have to change the way they think, how they manage their emotions, and have greater insights into their beliefs, drivers, values and attitudes. They may also have to change the way they deal with other people.

To achieve such deep, personal change I needed to understand the nature of the learning which created the person in the first place. The Mind Fit process predominantly uses implicit (natural) learning (e.g. Berry, 1997), which creates tacit knowledge. Knowledge about 'how to' do something which we are largely unaware (Polyani, 1958). Explicit learning, which I call educated learning, is the knowledge input provided to people by educationalists, trainers and work mentors, in or for organisations.

Renee Fuller (1999) compares the difference between implicit and explicit learning whilst Carol A Seger of Colorado University and Vivek Prabhakaran, Russell A Poldrack and John D E Gabrieli (2000) from Stanford University looked at the neural difference between the two forms of learning.

Implicit learning has been characterised as a passive process, where people are exposed to experiences, information, ideas and through observing, and acquire knowledge of 'how to' do something simply through that exposure. Explicit learning, on the other hand, is characterised as a process where people seek out the structure of any information that is presented to them sometimes in the form of theories. Psychologists suggest that much of the information learned during the normal course of life is learned implicitly, not explicitly. They cite activities such as language learning, riding a bike, social interactions and other complex activities, as examples of implicit learning. These are activities that people can do, but that they cannot explain how they do them.

Learning implicitly happens to all of us all the time. Without knowing it we copy people, cultures and working practices. Most of us have a desire to fit in wherever we are. We comply and conform effortlessly. And of course, most people's internal and external behaviours become a range of habits, some good and others not. This unwitting learning of what to be and what to do sits at the heart of learning to be helpless, defensive or powerful.

Recognising the powerful impact and influence of implicit learning, the Mind Fit process seeks to raise awareness our underlying beliefs, attitudes and habits. This enables us to explore this unconscious learning, to self assess and make a choice about what we want to do in the future. The process also seeks to give us experiences which mimic the circumstances in which we originally learned the dysfunctional habits.

The use of explicit learning during or mixed in with the Mind Fit process was found to interfere with and block implicit learning.

Today, we know that we can learn naturally to develop a whole range of strengths and weaknesses. They include courage, persistence and openness, or hopelessness, apathy and cynicism. Some excellent work by Paul T P Wong from Toronto University in 1995 and much later looked at persistence and flexibility which demonstrated how important these learnt strengths are for building success and improving performance.

Developing the concept of Mind Fitness

It is self-evident that while we may come equipped with some very effective instinctive ways of behaving, we need to know what is going on here if we are to make the best use of our innate and learned assets. Without this, Learned Helplessness may occur.

Learned Helplessness

One of the giants in this field of study is Martin Seligman. Seligman was interested in the way people think about and interpret events that befall them. They do this in order to make sense of their world. He called this our 'explanatory' style. This has three main dimensions:

- Permanence (stable)

- Pervasiveness (global)

- Personalisation (internal)

People who have learnt to be helpless have, in effect, learnt to focus, mainly unconsciously, on negative events, and to think of them in these terms: 'Bad events will last a long time, and no matter what I do, they won't go away, and it's my fault'.

Seligman described Learned Helplessness as:

> **'An apathetic attitude stemming from the conviction that one's actions do not have the power to effect one's situation.'**

Such people have learnt to believe that what happens in the world, or at work, or in their personal life, is always bad and those bad events are outside of their control. These kinds of beliefs dominate their mindset and are clearly dysfunctional and inhibit performance.

Learned Defensiveness®

While Learned Helplessness can often be seen in work and in other settings, I realised that it is not the only kind of dysfunctional set of beliefs and attitudes that people can have. For example, when a person has learnt consciously or unconsciously to protect themselves from what they perceive as a potential attack on their self image, I call it Learned Defensiveness®.

Learned Defensiveness®, a term which originated during the research, is similar to Learned Helplessness but instead of adopting an internalised view of the cause of negativity, people externalise it. Once again, the three main components are:

- Permanence (stable)—bad events will last a long time

- Pervasiveness (global)—they are everywhere

- Personalisation (externalise)—but it's not my fault

One of the underpinning characteristic of Learned Defensiveness® is that people feel vulnerable. As a result, they often tend to over-control situations in which they find themselves. Once their vulnerability is exposed they can quickly become helpless.

Learned Powerfulness®

In contrast to a sense of helplessness or defensiveness, Learned Powerfulness® is based on a very different set of beliefs. In fact, Seligman described them as similar states as Learned Optimism and authentic happiness, each flowing from a focus on positive events. Learned Powerfulness® has a very positive explanatory style consisting of:

- Permanence (stable)—good events will last a long time

- Pervasiveness (global)—will be frequent

- Personalisation (internal)—I make them happen

As a result, Personally Powerful people view setbacks as rare and see them as a new challenge to persist more or do something differently. They are very much in control of their performance.

Other researchers have also looked at this positive and optimistic state. Tali Sharot, author of The Optimism Bias, suggests that we are hardwired to be optimistic. In an article in the Observer newspaper (1/1/2012), she states that 76% of respondents to a questionnaire were optimistic about the future, even during these uncertain economic times. She suggests that being optimistic enables us to plan ahead, to save resources and work for future rewards. It also lets us forecast how our current behaviour may influence future generations.

Martin Seligman (2002) later developed Authentic Happiness from optimism. He based happiness on having three things in place: positive emotions, engagement and meaning. In 2011 he published a book entitled Flourish in which he added two more components to happiness. They are achievements and positive relationships.

In 2010 Jessica Pryce-Jones book entitled Happiness at Work links happiness to achieving potential. She suggests that the five core factors of happiness are contribution, conviction, culture, commitment and confidence.

Mind Fitness and other science

Learning to be Mind Fit embraces all these different views starts early in life. Neuroscience supports the view that early beginnings really make a difference. The work of Elizabeth Gould of Princeton University (1999) on primates, overturned the central tenet of neuroscience when she discovered that primate brains are constantly creating neurons and that they not only function but also respond to the environment. Her findings are significant and provide a link between the environment, neuroscience and genetics.

The most prolific development of brain neurons may take place during early childhood as new experiences create new circuits which, in turn, with use speed up and become stronger and more permanent. This is how we develop new strengths by using our brain. This process takes place all of our lives. But the links can fade away if we do not use it.

Walter Mischel (1970s) conducted experiments with children where he left them with a bell and a marshmallow. If they rang the bell he would return and they could eat the marshmallow. Alternatively, if they waited until he returned, they would receive an additional marshmallow. Some ate the marshmallow immediately he left the room. Some tried to put off the inevitable by distracting themselves for a period but eventually succumbed. Others were able to demonstrate personal control and resisted temptation and were rewarded with the second treat. Personal control was at the core of this experiment.

In follow-ups fourteen years later, he found those children who waited for the additional reward went on to achieve higher education results, went to better colleges and became better adults. These experiments, along with every-day experiences, tell us that self-control is one very important part of Mind Fitness. And that Mind Fitness is closely related to our ability to perform well in every sphere of our lives.

Roy F. Baumeister's work on will-power, published in the Psychologist, February 2012, describes self-control as the moral muscle. His states how psychologists over recent decades repeatedly showed that one of the most important strengths for helping people lead happy, successful and useful lives is self-control. He states, 'Self-control processes link together mind and body, present with future and past, resisting temptation with making choices, and a wide range of daily activities with each other'.

He goes on to say 'that when people exert self control, they use up some of their energy, leaving them in a depleted state'. This is why it is important to manage our personal energy and recognise that staying in control and focused is not sustainable. We need time to recuperate in the same way we do following physical exercise. He linked the levels of glucose in the body to self-control. So someone who makes lots of decisions, such as a judge or a manager, will deplete their glucose energy levels during the day. We need time to recover otherwise our decisions at the end of the day will be less thought through than at the start.

Collating the science into a new approach

The total research carried out, which looked at over 100 theories and models, is not simply a synthesis of existing work. It builds on and consolidates the understanding which has been built up over the previous quarter of a century, and offers a coherent way of thinking about what people need to do psychologically if they are to function well in challenging circumstances.

Whilst Seligman's work on belief systems was a powerful way to understand the concepts of Learned Helplessness, Defensiveness and Optimism, it was not the whole story. It was this recognition which led to the concept of Learned Powerfulness®.

For years I have suspected that people who have dysfunctional beliefs may be dysfunctional in other ways too. And of course—the opposite should also be true. This led to the decision to look at other areas of our psychological makeup.

Psychologists think of both the conscious and unconscious self, and within these, a number of quite separate but interlinked subsystems. The four psychological domains, which I call our four selves, are:

- The thinking self—collecting, processing and storing data.

- The feeling self—understanding and managing emotions and moods.

- The driving self—belief systems, value systems, motivators and attitudes.

- The social self—empathy and social skills.

Some of these domains you will already be very familiar to you as IQ (thinking self) and EQ (feeling self). Today, the driving self is often referred to as SQ (spiritual intelligence) and social self is also as known as SQ (social intelligence).

I think of Mind Fitness as a holistic concept, encompassing all these intrapersonal and interpersonal domains. The definition which I helped develop is as follows:

> **'Mind Fitness is a learned ability to function optimally in all psychological domains, thus enhancing performance in the pursuit of valued outcomes.'**
> **(Beggs and Williams, 2006)**

The thinking self

A number of areas were explored including thinking errors (Beck, 1976) and movement that takes place within the cortical function (e.g. Popper and Eccles, 1972). For any of us to be Mind Fit, we need to be aware of, and avoid thinking of errors, and to be aware of, and change narrow thinking preferences (e.g. Benziger, 1996; Sternberg, 1997).

Typical of work on thinking preferences is the Herman Brain Dominance Inventory (HBDI). This draws on the brain physiology research of Nobel prize-winning scientists like Roger Sperry and Michael Gazzaniga. It was developed by the late Ned Herrmann at General Electric using advanced brain scanning technology. The HBDI model has been validated by more than 60 doctoral theses and scientific studies, and by the satisfaction of more than 300,000 participants.

Work by Herrmann International shows that there are an equal number of people in all four basic groups of thinking—detailed, structured, harmonious, or as I refer to it as people thinking, and imaginative thinking. The four quadrant whole brain thinking model allows for sophisticated combinations that measure both intellectual and emotional preferences which influence thinking styles and learning styles.

Attention and distraction

The concept of metacognitive skills or the act of thinking about thinking, those personal support strategies closely associated with performance in several areas (e.g. Covington, 1985; Richardson, 1978), is also important. Many people fail to plan, prioritise etc.

Nideffer's (1976) work on Attentional Style led us to think about attention preferences. It is the cognitive process of paying attention to one particular aspect in the environment and ignoring others. Many people get locked into a too detailed style, and miss the big picture—or stay locked inside their head, listening to self-talk or drifting off to another time or place. A Mind Fit person understands this, and is able to shift attention as required.

A recent suggestion by Tipper (2005) proposes that we are designed to be distracted. In prehistoric times, any unexpected noise or smell may have been personally threatening. At the first sign of any perceived threat, we would therefore try and ascertain what it is; whatever we were focusing on is immediately removed from conscious awareness. While this once made good sense, today's world of distractions inevitably interfere with what we should be doing. We end up listening to other people's conversations, or responding to the 'ping' of an email message or thinking of where else we would like to be.

Acknowledging this and learning how to return our focus to what we are doing is an important component in Mind Fitness. Focusing on what is important can make such a difference yet maintaining focus is something we also appear to be programmed not to do. Gabriel Radvansky in The Psychologist (January 2012) suggests that we can lose our short term or working memory simply by moving from room to room.

That does not mean we cannot maintain focus if we choose to. Athletes do it for long periods as do people who have completed an advanced driving course. It just takes focused effort on what is important and it can be learnt quite quickly. If we can achieve focus, then we can enter the state of 'Flow'.

Being highly aware of what you are doing and by focusing on what is in your control ensures that your performance is improved.

The feeling self

I use the term feelings instead of emotions because feelings are what people say they experience; emotions are not always in conscious awareness.

Feeling awareness and competence has only come into general acceptance in recent times (e.g. Lane and Schwartz, 1987; Salovey and Mayer, 1990; Goleman, 1996) although they have been part of psychology from the beginning. An increase in Mind Fitness will not happen without some basic emotional understanding. This was acknowledged by Mayer and Salovey (1997), who presented a four-branch model of Emotional Intelligence. In this they speak of:

- The perception, appraisal and expression of emotion.

- Emotional facilitation of thinking.

- Understanding and analysing emotions; employing emotional knowledge.

- Reflective regulation of emotions to promote emotional and intellectual growth.

In Mind Fit workshops, it was apparent that many people had great difficulty in identifying feelings let alone being able to express them. By making explicit the relationship between bodily sensations, the underlying physiology and the experience of emotions proved a good way to bring feelings to the fore. Being able to name feelings that people experience and having some ideas of their physical and cognitive impact was a major step forward for many people. It constituted a step change in their Mind Fitness.

However, it is the control of feelings which was always going to be more important. Lazarus and Folkman's (1984) work on coping strategies focused on those all embracing cognitive skills which have become familiar in applications such as sport psychology, and cognitive behavioural therapy (CBT) developed for clinical work. By expanding conscious effort and through the use of personal tools to solve personal and interpersonal problems, you can master your feelings.

The differences between positive coping strategies or tools, versus non coping strategies used by people, is a rich source of differences which can be mapped onto levels of Mind Fitness quite intuitively. When this is done participants gain a deep insight into the way they currently function emotionally, and then find themselves in a position to choose to do things differently in the future.

Many coping 'tools' to deal with negative feelings originated from a variety of sources including coaching, Transactional Analysis, and Neuro Linguistic Programming (NLP). Other sources that focused on building a range of positive tools and were easily assessable to the participant were included. Many of these sources proved to be the participants themselves.

The driving self

Beliefs

Personal construct psychology (Kelly, 1955; Bannister and Fransella, 1986) made it clear that there is a need to consider beliefs under three headings:

- Beliefs about the self.

- Beliefs about the world and how it works.

- Beliefs about how to operate in the world.

A Mind Fit person has a belief system which creates a clear and positive view of themselves, a balanced view of the world, and allows the selection of effective attitudes and behaviours. As well as academic sources, to gain a broader understanding of beliefs I also turned to Transactional Analysis (Stewart and Joines, 1987) and Neuro Linguistic Programming (NLP) (Grinder and Bandler, 1976; Knight, 1995) to find ideas and tools which focus on beliefs and values.

Self efficacy beliefs

In 1977, with the publication of 'Self-efficacy: Toward a Unifying Theory of Behavioural Change,' Albert Bandura identified one kind of self-belief. For Bandura, self efficacy refers to the confidence in one's ability to behave in such a way as to produce a desirable outcome.

As he explained (Bandura 1997):

> **'Perceived self-efficacy refers to belief in one's agentive capabilities that one can produce given levels of attainment. A self-efficacy assessment, therefore, includes both an affirmation of a capability level and the strength of that belief.'**

Crucially, these beliefs are situation and context dependent. Self efficacy beliefs, unlike personality characteristics, are simply positive beliefs about one's capabilities to perform well in a given situation. These self-efficacy beliefs determine how people feel, think, motivate themselves and behave. As Bandura pointed out in 1994:

'There is a growing body of evidence that human accomplishments and positive well-being require an optimistic sense of personal efficacy. In sum, the successful, the venturesome, the sociable, the non-anxious, the non-depressed, the social reformers, and the innovators take an optimistic view of their personal capabilities to exercise influence over events that affect their lives. If not unrealistically exaggerated, such self-beliefs foster positive well-being and human accomplishments.'

Attribution theory

Attribution theory is closely linked to beliefs. It was developed over time from the theories of Fritz Heider (1958), Edward Jones Keith Davies, Harold Kelley (1967), and Lewis and Daltry (1990). It describes how people explain the successful or unsuccessful outcomes of their activities to one of four causes or attributions.

1. They did or did not put a lot of **effort** into the activity.

2. They did or didn't have the **ability** to do the activity.

3. The level of **task difficulty** was easy or hard.

4. They were **lucky** or they were not lucky.

Attributions can often be dysfunctional, and will result in lack of persistence or low motivation. It can lead to Learned Helplessness and Learned Defensiveness®.

Expectations

Beliefs are those things we already hold as true either now, or in the past, whilst expectations are our beliefs about the future. If what we desire or expect to happen is in conflict with what we believe we can or cannot achieve, we can experience internal conflict, known as cognitive dissonance. I may, for example, want to drive an Aston Martin, but believe I will never be able to earn enough money to buy one. Festinger, L. A. Theory of Cognitive Dissonance, Stanford University Press, Stanford, CA, 1957 outlines this state very clearly.

This uncomfortable internal state associated between two conflicting beliefs or expectations can be increased or decreased according to how important the subject matter is to us. The strength of the internal conflict and our ability to rationalise it also play a part. This internal strife can act as a personal demotivator. Conversely, the opposite is true. Clearly, this has implications for decision making at work and at home.

Drivers (or motivators)

Mainstream psychology has never really got to grips with the concept of human needs, tending to think in cognitive terms (Festinger, 1954) and expectancy theory (Vroom, 1964). None of these seemed to fit with reality. This led to revisiting established theories. One of the best known is Maslow's (1954) Hierarchy of Needs, which has not been well supported by evidence (e.g. Wahba and Bridgewell, 1976).

Recently, the most useful way of thinking about human needs came not from a psychologist at all, but from an economist. Max-Neef (1991). He suggested nine universal drivers:

- Subsistence

- Protection

- Affection

- Understanding

- Participation

- Recreation

- Creation

- Identity

- Freedom

More importantly, he identified good and bad ways to satisfy these drivers. Mind Fit people tend to choose positive activities which 'satisfies' their personal drivers.

Values

The idea of basic human values has been exciting psychologists for many years, from Allport, Vernon & Lindzey in 1931, to the present day. The debate has often been informed by thinking in other fields, such as moral philosophy, sociology and even religion.

Kluckhohn and Strodtbeck (1961) argued that there are a limited number of common human problems for which all people must at all times find some solution. In other words, values are the way in which we deal with, and reduce the apparent complexity of our world.

Later workers, such as Rokeach (1979) Hofstede (1980, 2001) and Schwartz (1992), came up with some basic value dimensions, and it is believed that psychologists are close to reaching a universally applicable theory of values.

Values used in the development of Mind Fitness are simply a set of behaviour codes—we should behave 'like this' in our dealings with the world, especially with others (cf. Bardi and Schwartz, 2003).

Attitudes

Attitudes are a construct with a positive or negative view of an experience, belief, idea, object, person, behaviour or event. They have an affective (emotional) response, a behavioural (action) intention and a cognitive (thinking) response. They can make you susceptible to certain kinds of stimuli and ready to respond in a fixed way. Attitudes undoubtedly drive our behaviour.

Zimbardo (1999) defined attitudes as a positive or negative evaluation of people, objects, events, activities, ideas, i.e. just about anything in your environment.

Attitudes are understood or implied without being stated. They may have an impact on our social self, perhaps surfacing as prejudices towards certain individuals or groups.

Other sources for this section include Fazio, R. (1990), Snyder, M. (1982), Erikson, B. (1998), Heider (1958) and Hovland, Janis and Kelly (1953)

The social self

Good interpersonal skills are important if we are to connect effectively with others. Performance coaching (Whitmore, 1996), which is largely based on the Rogerian principles of client-centred therapy, describes the kind of skills and mindset which can have a major impact on communication effectiveness. These include unconditional positive regard, empathic listening, the use of open questions, and a focused way to control the progress of a conversation.

The crucial factor is the effect on others which given interpersonal skills create. One of the non-mainstream approaches which addresses this is Transactional Analysis (e.g. Stewart and Joines, 1987).

Recently, social intelligence has been addressed by major players in the field including Daniel Goleman, Karl Albrecht and Margaret Hall. The ability to operate competently in a social setting depends to a surprising degree on understanding and managing our other selves: thinking, feeling and driving. For example, our unconscious attitudes can affect our ability to accept people for their difference; our ability to express our values openly helps to inspire and engage others; and by controlling our emotional state, we can improve our ability to empathise.

The complex self

A complex adaptive system (CAS) is not a pure theory. It is constructed from several theories based on relationships, emergent patterns and the act of repetition. CAS is all around us and includes the universe, the weather, immune systems and social systems, all of which are constantly adapting to their environment.

The Personal Profile Map® with its four selves can be described as a complex adaptive system (CAS) (Dooley 1997, Guastello 1995; Stacey 1996). What is missing from the map and which underpins it, is the plethora of mutual connections between the strengths and weaknesses, showing how they can affect each other. Changes to any one may have an effect on others.

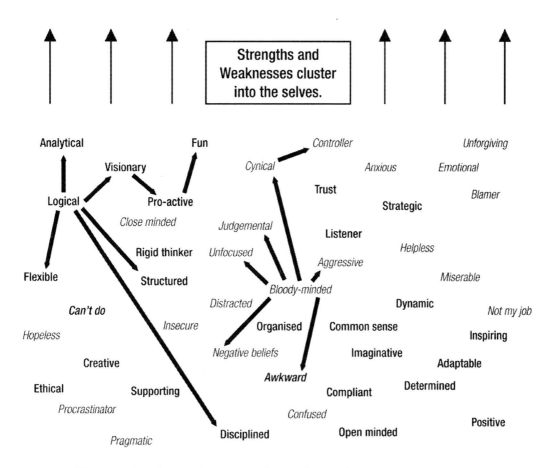

Diagram showing random strengths leading to 6 arrows and dialogue box

Guastello defined a CAS:

> **'A CAS behaves/evolves according to three key principles: order is emergent as opposed to predetermined, the system's history is irreversible, and the system's future is often unpredictable.'**

This sounds remarkably like the psychology of most people. Interestingly, the adaptations occur because the whole is made up from a number of discrete, but inter-relating parts, just as the model depicts. Guastello again:-

> **'The basic building blocks of the CAS are agents. Agents are semi-autonomous units that seek to maximize some measure of goodness, or fitness, by evolving over time.'**

The agents relating to Mind Fitness are strengths and weaknesses. Becoming Mind Fit simply means tuning up small parts of this complex system. This can only happen if an individual is aware of the nature of the system, their system, and the many ways that the strengths and weaknesses interact. Then we can find ways to optimise the various links both within and between the strengths and weaknesses.

For me, the whole of this psychological system is focused on achieving performance in the real world. And in our workshop experience, we consistently find that a small change in one part of Mind Fitness can have a large impact—exactly as the non-linearity of a complex system would predict.

Strengths and talents

A huge market is currently being created as organisations seek to identify the natural talents of their people and turn them into strengths. At the current time, there are several competing theories about strengths.

When one reads the literature on strengths, there is a curious sense that most people believe that somehow strengths are 'in there' waiting to be developed and used. For example, according to Buckingham and Clifton of the Gallup organisation, in their book 'The Strengths Revolution' they say:

> **'[Organisations] must watch for clues to each employee's natural talents and then position and develop each employee so that his or her talents are transformed into strengths. By changing the way it selects, measures, develops and channels the careers of its people, this revolutionary organisation must build its entire enterprise around the strengths of each person'**

This notion that talents are lying dormant, just waiting to be turned into skills, strengths or exceptional ability has already been dismissed by Howe, Davidson and Sloboda (1998) who conducted a wide-ranging examination of the evidence for this idea. K Anders Ericsson work on deliberate practice supports this idea. Howe, Davidson and Sloboda conclude that

> **'An analysis of positive and negative evidence and arguments suggests that differences in early experiences, preferences, opportunities, habits, training and practice are the real determinants of excellence [strengths]'**

In other words—the innate talent hypothesis is dead in the water. Talents do not turn into strengths; and on the whole, they do not appear to be genetically determined.

Research in the 21st century is supporting this view. For example, David Shenk in his book 'The genius in all of us' says that we develop through a gene-environment interaction with the environment predominately driving the change. A change in our environment, real or perceived, causes a protein to switch on the relevant gene which in turn, produces the hormone or whatever is needed at that moment in time, enabling a response.

Much of this thinking around talents and strengths is based on the premise that strengths measures can be used as a way to select people for specific jobs, and of course selection testing is an industry in its own right, with its own agenda to promote. Carol Dweck considers an additional downside of this approach to identifying talents/strengths. In her view, it may lead to a select, talented few deeming themselves somehow 'superior'. Of course, this attitude will only reinforce disengagement in the majority of the 'less talented' people.

More recently, Linley and Harrington, (2006) seem to have embraced the innate strengths notion, although they also acknowledge that strengths can be developed, or dormant strengths revived. They define strengths as:

> **'A natural capacity for behaving, thinking or feeling in a way that allows optimal functioning or performance in the pursuit of valued outcomes.'**

The research by Gallup on strengths is extensive but it is made up of qualitative interviews and according to David Sharpley, Chartered Psychologist, Gallup's work needs to be analysed quantitatively. Without this the research lacks depth.

The debate goes on.

For me, strengths are the outcome of both our innate assets and a learnt process which I call Mind Fitness. I have suggested that the key to exceptional performance is a sense of one's Personal Powerfulness, and propose that this is made up from two sources—beliefs in one's *capability* to perform, and beliefs in one's *capacity* to deal with the 'real world'—or Mind Fitness. These are what are currently called self-efficacy beliefs and strengths. I link this to the work outlined earlier in this chapter by Elizabeth Gould on neuron growth.

Therefore, I define strengths in this way

> **'Strengths are empowering beliefs about our ability to utilise our innate assets and effective learned personal strategies which contribute to our psychological capacity to perform.' (Beggs and Williams, 2007)**

This approach is very different from the current talent/strengths route and provides a means for a majority of people to excel. Experience also informs us that we can build strengths, or positive beliefs about people's capacity to perform. And I have seen how this can transform performance on a myriad of occasions.

By enabling individuals to identifying not only the individual strengths they need, but by placing strengths in clusters required to fulfil a task or role, then the individual has a common purpose to develop their strengths.

Leadership

Although the focus of this book is Mind Fitness because of underperformance, disengagement, conflict and stress in the workplace, I have also made reference to leaders and teams. It is quite simple, team members need to be Mind Fit as do leaders if productivity and success in this period of economic uncertainty is to be achieved.

In many ways, leadership style reflects how Mind Fit a leader is or isn't, and how reliant they are on various forms of power. They include expert power, positional power, the power of information and relationship power to achieve their business objectives. Amongst other things, leadership is an attitude and a relationship that involves both 'being' and 'doing', not just 'knowing'. The best leaders value their team members, act as a beacon for them and know how to draw outstanding contributions from them. These leaders use Personal Power.

One example of leadership which we have linked to Personal Power comes from Bass and Alvolio (1994) who described some of the characteristics of what they called Transformational Leaders. In this country, Professor Beverly Alimo-Metcalf's research has identified similar characteristics in leaders from both the public and private sectors (Alimo-Metcalf and Alban-Metcalf, 2001).

Transformational Leadership is not just about behavioural competencies, but also about something more fundamental—the qualities (or strengths) of the leader.

Teams

It is sometimes difficult to understand why some groups of people come together as a team and achieve their goals quickly and efficiently whilst others are doomed from the start with never ending conflict and apathy. Classical thinking on teams has it that teams go through a series of linear stages before they start performing, with each person carrying out their preferred role.

There are three main ideas relating to how teams develop: vertical, cyclical and random. Tuckman's classic vertical model, forming, storming, norming and performing has proved popular with trainers. However, as Tuckman acknowledged way back in 1962, the theory needed to be tested in the real world as the people on whom the theory was based were psychology students and people suffering from psychotic disorders or alcohol or chemical abuse. It was never robustly tested but is still found in common use today by trainers.

In fact, there are many real life examples of teams that form and immediately perform; they seem not to go through Tuckman's stages at all. The stage of storming is not compulsory and will not occur if team members are Mind Fit

The cyclical models suggest that every time a change occurs, for instance, when the team task changes or a new member joins, it upsets the balance and it reverts to an earlier state. One example of a cyclical model is when a person joins a team as they are initially very dependent on their colleagues. Next, they seek to become independent and finally, in the best performing teams, team members become interdependent. Again, this may or may not happen depending on how Mind Fit or mind UN-Fit people are.

The random models suggest exactly that. Teams are at varied states depending on the mindset of members, their tasks and the context in which they operate. In today's world of different types of teams, whether it is office based or virtual, the constant challenges will be on-going and any model that suggests stability is not synchronised with reality.

I often liken an organisational team to an Olympic team. Countries' representatives are all members of the big team. Athletes may participate in team sports such as hockey or volleyball whilst others will be part of a relay team—each doing their own bit and then handing the batten over to a colleague. Others will compete individually in their own sport such as archery or boxing.

This view of teams and team working resonates more closely with what actually takes place in organisations today.

Of course, Mind Fitness does not rely on knowledge of theories. However, if you would like to discover more I have selected a range of books which cover many of the areas above. These are listed in Appendix C.

CHAPTER 11

Completing The Jigsaw

Quote: 'The world is a dangerous place, not because of those who do evil, but because of those who look on and do nothing.' Albert Einstein

It is time to do something different if we are going to develop successful people and build successful businesses. Doing what we have always done is no longer an option.

Businesses need to raise their game in light of the new challenges that the change in the economic environment has caused. The future is very unpredictable. Some of the best minds in the world of finance are struggling to solve the Euro crises. They make recommendations and then within hours or days the solutions are in tatters. Markets seem to have a mind of their own. Trust is at an all time low when it comes to lending money. Banks say they lend but the perception is that they do not to the level needed to stimulate the economy.

So to ensure that you and your business are ready for the challenge you need to think, then think again. Ask yourself:

- 'Am I Mind Fit?'

- 'Does my workplace operate in a Mind Fit way?'

- 'Is my Business Fit?'

- 'Am I and my people Knowledge Fit?'

- 'Do all the parts fit together?'

Most people have little control over the international situation or those larger events that continually appear in the news. We can only control our part of it by making sure all the components of a successful business are in place. If enough of us do this then we can make a difference. Whether this is in our local community, a city, a region or nationally, if enough people think about their businesses in a Mind Fit way we can become more productive, more lean, more energised and more profitable. This means more jobs, particularly for young people, more money in circulation and an increased sense of well being.

Business Fit

We all know what we should have in place to ensure that our business will thrive. But have you?

- Have you put in place all those parts that you need to have to be Business Fit?

- Do you have a clear purpose from which to build your business plan?

- Are the sales and marketing strategies realistic and workable?

- Do you have the required support in place that may include HR and training, health and safety, procedures and policies?

- Are they agile, flexible and adaptable plans and processes for continual change?

By ensuring that all the component parts link together in an agile yet realistic and practical way, and you have a monitoring and measuring system in place, then you are Business Fit.

Knowledge Fit

Knowledge is generally made up of two core components. The technical knowledge that people need to perform their role whether as an engineer, accountant or IT specialist are usually in place in a majority of organisations. The second element of knowledge is where it falls down. As I have repeatedly mentioned this refers to training that provides knowledge for soft skills. These include personal effectiveness, team working and leadership, handling conflict and time management. The transference of the knowledge relating to these is known to be poor. It has been estimated that this form of knowledge transfer into action is between 0% and 20%.

The reason is that people are given theories and concepts which are interesting but not easily transferable making the input unusable. It is therefore a costly exercise and a waste of time. Many people are also Mind UN-Fit so do not have the drive to change.

Knowledge must be relevant, accurate and usable. If you ensure it is by challenging training providers before any intervention takes place then what you and your people receive should be measurable by way of activity and increases in productivity. If not, it is a waste of money.

- Have you ensured that the requisite level of technical training has been delivered to the people that need it when they need it?

- Have you ensured that the soft skills' training is relevant, accurate and usable?

- Have you measures in place as and when required, identifying attitude and behavioural changes and levels of staff engagement?

- Have you monitoring and measuring systems in place to show that your business processes are operating in a lean way and the output results are known?

One of the benefits of challenging the knowledge input and removing training which is not usable in the workplace or adds value to the business, it can significantly reduce an organisations abstraction rate and training budget. Why spend money on something that gives a poor return on investment.

Mind Fit

We must also be realistic. We cannot predict with any certainty what is going to happen, but one thing we can predict, is that if we do nothing we will struggle and, as a business, may not survive. People need to change their mindset, become more innovative, entrepreneurial, energised and focused. This is why the time has come for the third part of the jigsaw to be activated—Mind Fitness.

The Mind Fit journey is aimed simply at improving personal performance and business productivity. This final part of the jigsaw is the glue that businesses have been seeking. Put it into context of your world and the challenges that you face, at macro or micro levels, what difference would it make?

What difference will it make if you choose to ignore Mind Fitness?

The people issues that small businesses, large corporations or even governments face appear to be similar across the world. They are hurting business performance and productivity. They also have a major negative impact on people and relationships.

Issues such as:

- Disengagement

- Poor leadership

- Personal ineffectiveness

- Team working

- Poor performance

- Wasted time

- Lack of focus

- Stress

- Conflicts

The application of Mind Fitness applies for any situation involving people. The process tackles these issues directly. As the book has demonstrated, Mind Fit people operate in an agile, positive and productive way—willingly.

The application of the Mind Fitness process in organisations is directly linked to the issues outlined above and to the business imperatives. Whatever role the organisation is engaged in, if it involves people, then Mind Fitness is applicable. The process has been applied in a wide range of organisations that include:

- Public sector

  o Police

  o Local authorities

- o National Health Service

- o Speech and language departments

- o HM court services

- Private sector

  - o International high tech industry

  - o Executive jet pilots

  - o International civil engineers

  - o Universities

  - o Pharmaceutical industry

  - o Major airline

  - o Financial sector

  - o Training consultancies

- Unemployed

- Individuals seeking personal growth

Mind Fitness has been used to develop people from the shop floor to chief executives and boards of directors. With individuals, teams and departments right through to organisations. What is surprising is that the changes that people make are invariably small but the impact can be huge. The fact is that the process works for people and organisations because it is directly linked to business needs. Changes to both attitude and behaviours can be measured as well as tangible results.

It works

In a manufacturing company which was heading for bankruptcy the intervention of a Mind Fit approach linked to the business challenges turned the company round in three months.

Here are some other examples of the type of output that has been achieved:

- White goods manufacturer—productivity increased by 65%.

- Local authority savings made in transport—£500,000.

- Meetings reduced by 60% and were more productive.

- Number of multimillion pound projects increased by 13%.

- Conversion of sales for training products increased by 50%.

- New initiative led to the recovery of £300,000.

- Civil engineers increased business and staff across the UK and opened up new offices.

- I.T. initiative in NHS hospital which was being delayed through inactivity was actioned successfully and within budget.

Whether the change relates to individuals, a team or a company the Mind Fit intervention applies to all. What difference would it make to you and your business if you achieved a 5% or 10% improvement?

The cleaner and the entrepreneur

The title sounds like it could be an intriguing story yet it is the same person. Suzie attended a Mind Fit workshop in 2008. She was really concerned because the other attendees were working in a variety of what she considered to be 'prestigious' roles, were experienced, and some had higher qualifications whilst she was 'just' a cleaner. Her confidence was low and she was not sure if it would benefit her. To her credit, with all that immense doubt, she persevered.

The workshops are designed to be insightful, to intrigue and create light bulb moments so that the participants started thinking differently and deeply. It provided some very practical tools. Suzie told me that by mid morning she had self assessed enough to realise that she had given away control to other people throughout her whole life. She had played a subservient role and that was the way it was for her.

At the end of the day she was not sure how to move things forward. She did not know if she could change. I said that it was simply a matter of breaking a bad and destructive habit and doing something different. She did not know what to do so I suggested that she took her watch off her left wrist and attach it to her right. She told me it felt really uncomfortable so I told her to email me when it felt natural. Four days later the email arrived. My next question was, 'What are you going to do next?'

Suzie embarked on a life changing journey by making a series of small changes. She renegotiated with her husband some of the financial control so she had more funds. She went to evening classes which eventually led to her taking part in a practical philosophy course. She learnt to debate, discuss, explore and her life changed. She attended ballet and opera performances. She became confident and was content with whom she was, although that kept changing.

She decided to follow one of her passions which was antiques and now runs a successful antique business. She uses the internet as a sales vehicle, attends antique fairs to buy and sell in Europe, and has a stand in an antique centre. Life became richer and fulfilling.

Three years later Suzie took part in a Mind Fit workshop as a top up. She said afterwards, 'Enjoyable and useful. It made me realise how much I have achieved since my first introduction to the Mind Fitness programme and how many of the 'tools' I still use almost on a daily basis as a matter of course without realising it. The skills I learned originally are still with me. As Graham said, "Like learning to ride a bike, once you have learnt to do it you cannot unlearn it". The refresher has spurred me on to achieve more—I believe I can if I want to.'

- What different would it make to you or your organisation if people operated from a 'can do' position?

- What difference would it make if more people had an agile, flexible and adaptable mindset in which to respond to constant change?

- What difference would it make if people persevered?

The Mind Fit process

The Mind Fit process is both simple and intuitively right. It is based on using our innate assets linked to those parts of the brain that are in our control: our thinking, our feelings, our beliefs and drivers, and how we communicate with other people. We need to increase our awareness of how we and other people operate in work or in other situations. Simply by focusing on those inputs that are important at that moment in time and learning from the experience will lead to increased performance and confidence.

The use of natural learning is very powerful as it is action based, automatic and takes place unconsciously. And we are in control of it when we apply focus. The results can be staggering.

All you need to carry with you in your head is:

- One map—the Personal Profile Map.

- The three states—'can't do', won't do' and 'can do'.

- The four selves—thinking, feelings, driving and social.

Virtually everything you or other people do can be fitted into the map. Being aware of which part you are operating from enables you to take control of what you think and do and focus on what is important at that moment in time. Feedback enables us to keep growing.

Stop trying to survive and start to thrive.

The successful business

The world post 2007 has changed beyond all recognition and is now very unpredictable. Rigid linear processes and systems with long term plans can no longer provide a consistent route to success. Businesses must become agile, flexible and adaptable, just like their people. Building a business around a clear purpose is essential. It gives meaning to people enabling them to part of it and provide that added value.

Leadership must change. Leaders need to be authentic, engaging and collaborative. To work in different timeframes and provide the context for their people. Leaders must not only inspire, but learn to involve, engage and empower. Leaders need to give power away and grow their people.

The completed jigsaw with all its component parts in place leads to a successful business. This can only be achieved if people are Mind fit. Mind Fitness is the prequel to other actions.

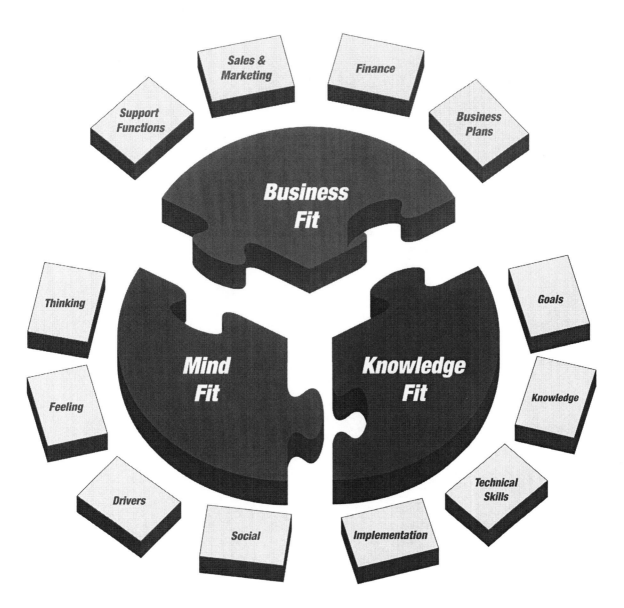

Taking the journey is easier than you think. So just do it.

The choice is yours.

Flow chart relating
to business performance

In 1959 a four point method for measuring training was outlined by Donald Kirkpatrick.

1. Reaction. Often referred to as a 'happy sheet'.

2. Learning achieved

3. Attitude and behavioural changes

4. Tangible results

For decades HR and training have focused on measuring Kirkpatrick's 1 and 2. Level 3 and 4 have mainly been ignored. Alliger &Janak (1989) research found a poor correlation between each level and in 2007 the CIPD stated that the transfer of learning back into the workplace was 'not much better than random chance'.

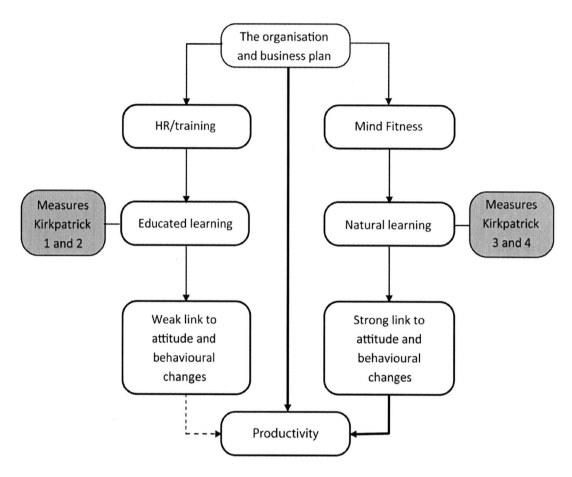

The Mind Fitness process directly seeks to link Kirkpatrick's levels 3 and 4 with the business and its imperatives that lead to success.

APPENDIX B

Strengths from providers referred to in the book

1. Strengthscope™ strengths (24) 2010

Collaboration:	You work with others to overcome conflict and build towards a common goal
Common sense:	You make pragmatic judgements based on practical thinking and previous experience
Compassion:	You demonstrate a deep and genuine concern for the well being and welfare of others
Courage:	You take on challenges and face risks by standing up for what you believe
Creativity:	You come up with new ideas and original solutions to move things forward
Critical thinking:	You approach problems and arguments by breaking them down systematically and evaluating them objectively
Decisiveness:	You make quick, confident and clear decisions, even when faced with limited information
Detail orientation:	You pay attention to detail in order to produce high quality output, no matter what the pressure
Developing others:	You promote people's learning and development to help them achieve their goals and fulfil their potential
Efficiency:	You take well ordered and methodical approach to tasks to achieve planned outcomes
Emotional control:	You are aware of your emotional triggers and how to control these to ensure you remain calm and productive
Empathy:	You readily identify with other people's situations and can see things clearly from their perspective
Enthusiasm:	Demonstrating passion and energy when communicating goals, beliefs, interests or ideas you feel strongly about

Flexibility:	You remain adaptable and flexible in face of unfamiliar or changing situations
Initiative:	You take independent action to make things happen and achieve goals
Leading:	You take responsibility for influencing and motivating others to contribute to the goals and successes of their team and organisation
Optimism:	Remaining positive and upbeat about the future and your ability to influence it to your advantage
Persuasiveness:	You are able to win agreement and support for a position or desired outcome
Relationship building:	You take steps to build networks of contacts and act as a 'hub' between people you know
Resilience:	You deal effectively with setbacks and enjoy overcoming difficult challenges
Result focus:	You maintain a strong sense of focus on results, driving tasks and projects to completion
Self-confidence:	You have a strong belief in yourself and your abilities to accomplish tasks and goals
Self-improvement:	You draw on a wide range of people and resources in pursuit of self-development and learning
Strategic mindedness:	You focus on the future and take a strategic perspective on issues and challenges

2. The VIA Classification of Character Strengths (updated Oct. 23, 2008)

Wisdom and Knowledge—Cognitive strengths that entail the acquisition and use of knowledge

- **Creativity** [originality, ingenuity]: Thinking of novel and productive ways to conceptualize and do things; includes artistic achievement but is not limited to it

- **Curiosity** [interest, novelty-seeking, openness to experience]: Taking an interest in ongoing experience for its own sake; finding subjects and topics fascinating; exploring and discovering

- **Judgment & Open-Mindedness** [critical thinking]: Thinking things through and examining them from all sides; not jumping to conclusions; being able to change one's mind in light of evidence; weighing all evidence fairly

- **Love of Learning:** Mastering new skills, topics, and bodies of knowledge, whether on one's own or formally; obviously related to the strength of curiosity but goes beyond it to describe the tendency to add systematically to what one knows

- **Perspective** [wisdom]: Being able to provide wise counsel to others; having ways of looking at the world that make sense to oneself and to other people

Courage—Emotional strengths that involve the exercise of will to accomplish goals in the face of opposition, external or internal

- **Bravery** [valor]: Not shrinking from threat, challenge, difficulty, or pain; speaking up for what is right even if there is opposition; acting on convictions even if unpopular; includes physical bravery but is not limited to it

- **Perseverance** [persistence, industriousness]: Finishing what one starts; persisting in a course of action in spite of obstacles; "getting it out the door"; taking pleasure in completing tasks

- **Honesty** [authenticity, integrity]: Speaking the truth but more broadly presenting oneself in a genuine way and acting in a sincere way; being without pretence; taking responsibility for one's feelings and actions

- **Zest** [vitality, enthusiasm, vigor, energy]: Approaching life with excitement and energy; not doing things halfway or halfheartedly; living life as an adventure; feeling alive and activated

Humanity—Interpersonal strengths that involve tending and befriending others

- **Capacity to Love and Be Loved:** Valuing close relations with others, in particular those in which sharing and caring are reciprocated; being close to people

- **Kindness** [generosity, nurturance, care, compassion, altruistic love, "niceness"]: Doing favours and good deeds for others; helping them; taking care of them

- **Social Intelligence** [emotional intelligence, personal intelligence]: Being aware of the motives and feelings of other people and oneself; knowing what to do to fit into different social situations; knowing what makes other people tick

Justice—Civic strengths that underlie healthy community life

- **Teamwork** [citizenship, social responsibility, loyalty]: Working well as a member of a group or team; being loyal to the group; doing one's share

- **Fairness:** Treating all people the same according to notions of fairness and justice; not letting personal feelings bias decisions about others; giving everyone a fair chance.

- **Leadership:** Encouraging a group of which one is a member to get things done and at the time maintain time good relations within the group; organizing group activities and seeing that they happen.

Temperance—Strengths that protect against excess

- **Forgiveness & Mercy:** Forgiving those who have done wrong; accepting the shortcomings of others; giving people a second chance; not being vengeful

- **Modesty & Humility:** Letting one's accomplishments speak for themselves; not regarding oneself as more special than one is

- **Prudence:** Being careful about one's choices; not taking undue risks; not saying or doing things that might later be regretted

- **Self-Regulation** [self-control]: Regulating what one feels and does; being disciplined; controlling one's appetites and emotions

Transcendence—Strengths that forge connections to the larger universe and provide meaning

- **Appreciation of Beauty and Excellence** [awe, wonder, elevation]: Noticing and appreciating beauty, excellence, and/or skilled performance in various domains of life, from nature to art to mathematics to science to everyday experience

- **Gratitude:** Being aware of and thankful for the good things that happen; taking time to express thanks

- **Hope** [optimism, future-mindedness, future orientation]: Expecting the best in the future and working to achieve it; believing that a good future is something that can be brought about

- **Humor** [playfulness]: Liking to laugh and tease; bringing smiles to other people; seeing the light side; making (not necessarily telling) jokes

- **Religiousness & Spirituality** [faith, purpose]: Having coherent beliefs about the higher purpose and meaning of the universe; knowing where one fits within the larger scheme; having beliefs about the meaning of life that shape conduct and provide comfort

3. Gallup 34 strengths used in their Strengthfinder 2 questionnaire.

Achiever:	People strong in the Achiever theme have a great deal of stamina and work hard. They take great satisfaction from being busy and productive.
Activator:	People strong in the Activator theme can make things happen by turning thought into action. They are often impatient.
Adaptability:	People strong in the Adaptability theme prefer to 'go with the flow'. They tend to be 'now' people who take things as they come and discover the future one day at a time.
Analytical:	People strong in the Analytical theme search for reasons and causes. They have the ability to think about factors that might affect a situation.
Arranger:	People strong in the Arranger theme can organize, but they also have a flexibility that complements this ability. They like to figure out how all the pieces and resources can be arranged for maximum productivity.
Belief:	People strong in the Belief theme have certain core values that are unchanging. Out of these values emerges a defined purpose for their life.
Command:	People strong in the Command theme have a presence. They can take control of a situation and make decisions.
Communication:	People strong in the Communication theme generally find it easy to put thoughts into words. They are good conversationalist and presenters.
Competition:	People strong in the Competition theme measure their progress against the performance of others. They strive to win first place and revel in the contests.
Connectedness:	People strong in the Connectedness theme have faith in the links between all things. They believe there are few coincidences and that almost every event has a reason.
Consistency:	People strong in the Consistency theme are keenly aware of the need to treat people the same. They try to treat everyone in the world fairly by setting up clear rules and adhering to them.
Context:	People strong in the Context theme enjoy thinking about the past. They understand the present by researching its history.

Deliberative:

People strong in the Deliberative theme are best described by the serious care they take in making decisions or choices. They anticipate obstacles.

Developers:

People strong in the Developer theme recognise and cultivate the potential in others. They spot the signs of each small improvement and derive satisfaction from these improvements.

Discipline:

People strong in the Discipline theme enjoy routine and structure. Their world is best described by the order they create.

Empathy:

People strong in the Empathy theme can sense the feelings of other people by imagining themselves in the others' lives or others' situation.

Focus:

People strong in the Focus theme can take direction, follow through, and make corrections necessary to stay on track. They prioritise and then act.

Futuristic:

People strong in the Futuristic theme are inspired by the future and what they could be. They inspire others with their visions of the future.

Harmony:

People strong in the harmony theme look for consensus. They don't enjoy conflict; rather, they seek areas of agreement.

Ideation:

People strong in the Ideation theme are fascinated by ideas. They are able to find connections between seemingly disparate phenomena.

Inclusiveness/Includer:

People strong in the Inclusiveness theme are accepting of others. They show awareness of those who feel left out, and make an effort to include them.

Individualisation:

People strong in the Individualisation theme are intrigued with the unique qualities of each person. They have a gift for figuring out how people who are different can work together productively.

Input:

People strong in the Input theme have a craving to know more. Often they like to collect and archive all kinds of information.

Intellection:

People strong in the Intellection theme are characterized by their intellectual activity. They are introspective and appreciate intellectual discussions.

Learner:

People strong in the Learner theme have a great desire to learn and want to continuously improve. In particular, the process of learning, rather than the outcome, excites them.

Maximizer:	People strong in the Maximizer theme focus on strengths as a way to stimulate personal and group excellence. They seek to transform something strong into something superb.
Positivity:	People strong in the Positivity theme have an enthusiasm that is contagious. They are upbeat and can get others excited about what they are going to do.
Relator:	People who are strong in the Relator theme enjoy close relationships with others. They find deep satisfaction in working hard with friends to achieve goals.
Responsibility:	People strong in the Responsibility theme take psychological ownership of what they say they will do. They are committed to stable values such as honesty and loyalty.
Restorative:	People strong in the Restorative theme are adept at dealing with problems. They are good at figuring out what is wrong and resolving it.
Self-Assurance:	People strong in the Self-assurance theme feel confident in their ability to manage their own lives. They possess an inner compass that gives them the confidence that their decisions are right.
Significance:	People strong in the Significance theme want to be very important in the eyes of others. They are independent and want to be recognised.
Strategic:	People strong in the Strategic theme create alternative ways to proceed. Faced with any given scenario, they can quickly spot the relevant patterns and issues.
Woo:	People strong in the Woo theme love the challenge of meeting new people and winning them over. They derive satisfaction from breaking the ice and making connections with another person.

Author's recommended book list

Complexity	M Michael Waldrop (1992)
Learned helplessness	Martin Seligman (1993)
Implicit learning and tacit knowledge	Arthur S. Reber (1993)
Training & development sourcebook	Schneir, Russel, Beatty, Baird (1994)
The emotional brain	Joseph LeDoux (1996)
Finding flow	M Csikszenmihalyi (1997)
The soul at work	Roger lewin & Birute Regime (1999)
Awesome Purpose	Nigel MacLennan (1999)
Inner game of work	W Timothy Galwey (2000)
The feeling of what happens	Antonio Damasio (2000)
Spiritual intelligence	Danah Zohar & Ian Marshall (2000)
Managing the human animal	Nigel Nicholson (2000)
A psychology of human strengths	Aspinwall and Staudinger (2003
Positive psychology	Alan Carr (2004)
Social intelligence in everyday life	C Margaret Hall (2005)
The biology of belief	Bruce H. Lipton (2005)
Thriving mind	Katherine Benziger (2006)
Social intelligence	Karl Albrecht (2006)
Sudden influence	Michael A, Rousell (2007)
The brain that changes itself	Norman Doidge (2007)
Mindset	Carol S. Dweck (2008)
Talent is overrated	Geoff Colvin (2008)
The neuro revolution	Zack Lynch with Byron Laursen (2009)
Rewire your brain	John B Arden (2010)
Bounce	Matthew Syed (2010)
The genius in all of us	David Shenk (2010)
Happiness at work	Jessica Pryce-Jones (2010)
Choke	Sian Beilock (2010)
Flourish	Martin E P Seligman (2011)
3-Dimensional Leadership	Nigel Linacre & Jefferson Cann (2011)

Background to the author and Mind Fitness

Graham had a successful career in two police forces in the United Kingdom (UK) followed by a period as a performance coach in a variety of blue chip companies in the UK.

He first got involved in looking at alternative methods of training and development following the terrorist bomb in Deal, in the UK and the ferry disaster just off-shore near Zeebrugge, Belgium when nearly 200 people were killed. He was a senior police officer at the time. What first intrigued him was that most of the people who dealt with the worst of each situation did not suffer post traumatic stress disorder whilst some others, for instance, those who were on telephones, did. Why is this?

His curiosity got the better of him so he embarked on a hypnotherapy course and later became a psychotherapist. It was still not enough. He qualified as a counsellor and followed this up with transactional analysis, neuro-linguistic-programming (NLP), and other courses. He needed to know more.

Then in 1998 whilst working as a performance coach with former top sports professionals, he was asked to look at why the transfer of certain types of training and coaching back into the work place was relatively poor. Too many people attended training programmes and shortly afterwards, they returned to their old habits on their return to work. He was off on another journey, but this time he was stepping into new territory.

However, there is a lot of science out there to help the journey that eventually led him to explore neuroscience, biology and epigenetic. This journey is still ongoing.

What he discovered was that the key to success lay in a person changing their mindset, not knowledge. It may seem obvious, but the journey was not as simple as that. It has resulted in the Mind Fit process which turned the traditional training approach on its head. It is crucial to develop the mind before applying the knowledge.

Lightning Source UK Ltd.
Milton Keynes UK
UKOW012138231012

201072UK00001B/5/P